KEYNES AND THE CLASSICS

KEYNES AND THE CLASSICS

Edited with Introductions by
ROBERT LEKACHMAN
BARNARD COLLEGE

D. C. HEATH AND COMPANY · BOSTON

"He taught men to unite reason with hope. . . ."

HUGH DALTON

Boston • Englewood • Chicago • Dallas
San Francisco • Atlanta • London • Toronto

Library of Congress Catalog Card Number: 64–25794

Printed in the United States of America. (6 I 4)

CONTENTS

I. THE CASE FOR THE KEYNESIAN REVOLUTION

Introduction 1

JOHN MAYNARD KEYNES

What is classical economics? 3

What is "general" about the *General Theory?* 3

What are the classical postulates? How does the new principle of effective demand contradict them? 4

What is aggregate demand? What is aggregate supply? 18

How does the theory fit together? 20

MILTON FRIEDMAN

How has the *General Theory* stimulated economic research? 26

ALVIN H. HANSEN

Why is the consumption function a great contribution to economic theory? 30

PAUL M. SWEEZY

What has Keynes contributed to the analysis of capitalism? 33

II. THE CASE FOR KEYNESIAN CONTINUITY

Introduction 37

HARRY G. JOHNSON

How important is Cambridge to Keynesian economics? 39

BERTIL OHLIN

What did Knut Wicksell and his followers contribute to income theory? 43

In the light of Swedish theory, what is a fair judgment of Keynes? 49

A. P. LERNER

Why is Keynes' wage doctrine correct? 59

GOTTFRIED HABERLER

What are the errors in Keynes' wage theory and attack upon Say's Law? 64

SIR DENNIS ROBERTSON

Why is the Keynesian theory of interest erroneous? 73

GOTTFRIED HABERLER

In the light of an inadequate theory of interest, why is the Keynesian system less original and less useful than has been claimed? 77

III. THE OUTCOME

Introduction 81

JOHN WILLIAMS

How much of Keynes' originality was a matter of theory and how much of "opinion"? 82

DAVID McC. WRIGHT

Why Keynesianism is a weak doctrine in the modern world 88

MELVIN REDER

Why did Keynes really make a difference? 89

ROBERT LEKACHMAN

How useful is Keynes today? 93

SUGGESTIONS FOR READING 113

INTRODUCTION

The eminent American economist Paul Samuelson, who was a Harvard graduate student when John Maynard Keynes' *General Theory of Employment, Interest and Money* was published, has written of the excitement that the book caused and the good fortune that economists of his generation enjoyed because of their opportunity to grow up professionally during the Keynesian Revolution in economic theory. In Samuelson's words, "the *General Theory* caught most economists under the age of 35 with the unexpected virulence of a disease first attacking and decimating an isolated tribe of south sea islanders."

A generation has elapsed since Keynes startled both his colleagues and a wider public with new doctrines about unemployment, public works, national budgets, and, indeed, the appropriate subject matter of economics itself. It is fair to say that for most economists Keynes has been absorbed so thoroughly into the literature and the practice of their professions, that the question "Are you a Keynesian?" is almost irrelevant. Every important beginning textbook which is at all widely used in the United States contains chapters on national income, national income determination, and fiscal policy which were rarely to be found in textbooks published on the other side of the great Keynesian watershed. An historic milestone was approached in 1963 when a President, for the first time in our political record, deliberately proposed a tax reduction and a large accompanying peacetime deficit in the federal budget, on the good Keynesian ground that the economy required this particular stimulation, at this particular time. In economics this is the normal progression of an original idea: from its author, to other economists, from other economists to the textbooks, and finally from the textbooks to the public policies of democratically elected officials.

Surely then the *General Theory* — if we use it as a convenient shorthand expression of Keynes' total influence — was a book with an impact, comparable in force with Smith's *Wealth of Nations* and Ricardo's *Principles of Political Economy and Taxation.* Certainly economic policy is different, political alternatives are expanded, and the study of economics transformed because Keynes lived. But how much was this a matter of presentation, of style, and of bold claims for novelty? How much of the Keynesian message was, after all, a restatement of older doctrines which at last found an eager reception in the midst of a vast economic depression? On intellectual grounds are we better advised to view Keynes as a continuation, possibly a culmination of certain intellectual tendencies in English and Swedish economic thought, or should we think of a Keynesian "revolution," a revitalization of economic theory, and a fundamental shift in the outlook of economics?

In short, was Keynes, his own protestations to the contrary, essentially a "classical economist"? Definition must precede any attempt to answer this question. Keynes' own definition of "classical" covered "those . . . who adopted and perfected the theory of the Ricardian economics, including . . . J. S. Mill, Marshall, Edgeworth and Prof. Pigou." Now many other economists have taken the term "classical" to describe the characteristic doctrines of English economists from Adam Smith *through* John Stuart Mill. They have reserved the term "neo-classical" for the theories of Alfred Marshall and A. C. Pigou, Keynes' own Cambridge teachers. Nevertheless, Keynes' idiosyncratic definition contained its polemical advantages, for it enabled Keynes to associate contemporary economics with an earlier tradition which he endeavored to expose and discredit. As we proceed in this volume, the question "Was Keynes a Classical Economist?" will be handled in terms of his differences from or continuity with English Cambridge economists of the late 19th and early 20th century, primarily once again Alfred Marshall and A. C. Pigou. The context will make it plain when a different meaning of classical is in question.

The Case for Novelty

Keynes was an economist who did not read widely in the literature of his field. While he extended generous acknowledgments to predecessors when he was aware of their existence, he belonged securely to that school of Cambridge economists of whom it has been said that they preferred making things up to looking things up. Which is to say that Keynes was original both objectively and subjectively. What is the maximum case for his originality? In a social science like economics when in fact is something "new"? There are no analogues to the crucial experiments of physics available to economists. It appears that Keynes and his followers have made three distinguishable types of claims to originality.

First: The *General Theory* has a scope and an emphasis and hence a meaning which differ importantly from opposing doctrines. Indeed, such is the nature of the single claim made in the one paragraph first chapter of the *General Theory*.

Second: The *General Theory* is new because it destroys so much of older theories. This purely critical function in itself produces a different economics. As will appear, what Keynes attacks includes the venerable economic generalization termed Say's Law of Markets—the notion that unemployment is either voluntary or frictional, the idea that the rate of interest is a reward for postponing personal consumption, and the proposition that reducing wages will increase employment.

Third: Most important of all, the *General Theory* is novel because of what it substitutes for the theory which it demolishes. It replaces the conventional concentration upon individual prices and markets with an emphasis upon aggregates. For individual demand functions it substitutes an aggregate demand function, a consumption function, and a truly striking investment function. For conventional interest theory it substitutes liquidity preference. For the assumption of a tendency toward full employment it substitutes underemployment equilibrium. Finally for the neutral public finance of the past it substitutes the interventionist doctrines of modern fiscal theory. Perspectives, tools, and policies, all are altered.

Here then is the strongest case of discontinuity, for the proposition that Keynesian economics represents a break with an orthodox, classical tradition.

The Case for Continuity

One way to introduce the case for Keynes' anchorage in Cambridge economics is to indicate just how much he assumed that his opponents also accepted. Here at the outset of Chapter 18 is Keynes' somewhat belated statement of what he had been assuming in the first seventeen chapters:

We take as given the existing skill and quantity of available labour, the existing quality and quantity of available equipment, the existing technique, the degree of competition, the tastes and habits of the consumer, the disutility of different intensities of labour and of the activities of supervision and organisation, as well as the social structure including the forces, other than our variables set forth below, which determine the distribution of the national income." (page 245)

The statement's continuities are of two kinds. First is a continuity of the social order. Although there are stray remarks in fair numbers and even much of an entire late chapter (24) in the *General Theory* which can be interpreted as sympathetic to fundamental social and economic change, Keynes' analytical position embraces existing class relationships and the distribution of property and income upon which these relationships depend. In other words, his theory pertains to the same economic, social, and political order as Marshall's and Pigou's. Hence Keynes is in substantial disagreement with such dissident analyses of economic affairs as those of the Marxists and the Veblenians who assume alike the necessity and the inevitability of fundamental changes in the structure of property, income, and individual attitudes.

There is a second kind of continuity in Keynes: of technique, tools, and specific theories.

Technique

What does it mean to say that Keynes was a Cambridge economist? Among other things that he naturally followed the deductive technique which the Cambridge economists had themselves borrowed from their own predecessors, Ricardo and Mill. This technique requires those who use it to make simplifying assumptions about the character of economic reality, to exclude minor, frictional elements from their models, to reason from intuitively perceived first principles, and only gradually to reintroduce complicating elements. The long quotation from Keynes above fairly exemplifies the Keynesian reliance on the simplifying assumption. The importance to Keynes of *a priori,* deductive reasoning may be similarly illustrated by his analysis of the consumption function, the construction in Keynes which relates aggregate income to aggregate consumption. Here is the manner in which Keynes put the matter:

The fundamental psychological law upon which we are entitled to depend with great confidence both *a priori* from our knowledge of human nature and from the detailed facts of experience, is that men are disposed, as a rule, and on the average, to increase their consumption as their income increases, but not by as much as the increase in their income."

How does Keynes know this? By self-examination and by general observation. Now in economics the *a priori* assumption has a long history indeed, extending at the minimum from Adam Smith's assumption of a human "propensity to truck, barter, and exchange one thing for another" and his belief that "every individual is continually exerting himself to find out the most advantageous employment for whatever capital he can command," to Ricardo's confidence in rational profit maximization by businessmen, and Marshall's belief in the rational, allocating consumer. Thus Keynes' readiness to make *a priori* assumptions about human behavior was in the very best Cambridge tradition. Moreover, the content of these assumptions was not as far from tradition as Keynesians have sometimes believed. No doubt uncertainty, expectations, and "animal spirits" received considerably more emphasis in the *General Theory* than they did in "classical" texts. All the same, Keynes' businessmen and speculators were still busy at a familiar maximizing game and the basic analytical framework of the *General Theory* was no less static than Marshall and Pigou. It has been Keynes' successors, economists like Sir Roy Harrod, and Evsey Domar who have transformed the *General Theory* into a series of dynamic processes, focused upon economic growth.

Tools

There is only a single geometrical illustration to be found in the *General Theory*. Nevertheless, the early translators of Keynes encountered little trouble in converting the theory of income determination into plane geometry of extremely familiar countenance. The standard diagram which now pictures aggregative equilibrium in the Keynesian universe, often drawn in the manner of Figure 1, is simply an extension of the principles by which price is determined in competitive markets by the relationships of supply and demand. In the world of macroeconomics what is supplied is income and what is demanded is consumer and investment goods and services. But equilibrium is reached in essentially the same process of adjustment and any good Marshallian soon adjusts to the new labels and the new slopes of the curves. Tradition is as much preserved as it is violated in the macroeconomics of the new theories.

Specific Doctrines

Keynes said of the *General Theory* that ". . . the composition of this book has been for the author a long struggle of escape, and so must

FIGURE I

The Determination of Equilibrium Income

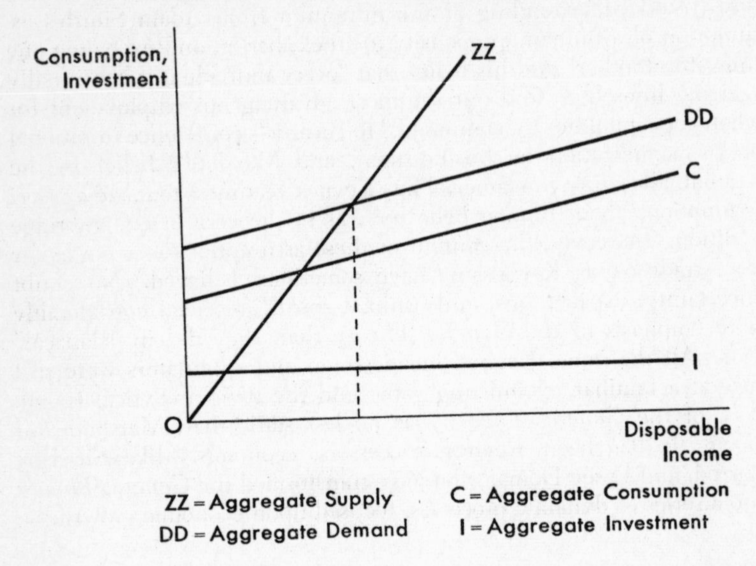

reading of it be for most readers." After all, did Keynes escape from as many of the old ideas as he hoped? In ideas priorities are tricky matters to settle. Often what counts more than the idea itself is the use to which it is put, the analytical system in which it is embedded. Thus marginal explanations of pricing are anticipated in Jeremy Bentham among others, but marginalism is a powerful theory associated with the 1870's because only then did Jevons, Walras, and Menger convert the insight into an alternative vision of the economic process. In other words, anticipations must be distinguished from coherent theories. Still, some of Keynes' antecedents did attain the dignity of coherent theories.

Take, as a leading case in point, the tangled relationship between saving and investment, a source of immediate controversy. In the *General Theory* Keynes' attitude amounted to the proposition that as accounting definitions saving and investment were always equal: aggregate consumption plus aggregate saving added to the same national income total as aggregate consumption plus aggregate investment. At the same time as Keynes advanced this impregnable identity, he also appeared to be saying something more. As the controversialists finally agreed, the something else was the proposition that saving and investment interpreted as summaries of the *intentions* rather than the actions of savers and investors, might and, indeed, usually did differ. When intended saving exceeded intended investment or vice versa, the process which brought them into equality involved a shift in income. Thus it was that the equilibrium level of income might correspond to a high level of unemployment. Viewed in this way, the Keynesian saving-investment hypothesis had important Swedish antecedents in the writings of Knut Wicksell and his Stockholm followers. It owed a good deal as well to the writings of the late Sir Dennis Robertson whose *Banking Policy and the Price Level,* published a full decade before the *General Theory,* made a series of important distinctions among the varieties of saving and investment and derived some processes from their relationships which were decidedly "Keynesian" in flavor.

Again, as Keynes himself generously admitted, the English dissident economist John A. Hobson had at the least anticipated the central Keynesian demonstration that underemployment equilibrium was possible and usual. Keynes was convinced that Hobson had anticipated much – "one half of the matter" – of his saving doctrine. Keynes thought that Hobson had vitiated his achievement only by the erroneous belief that excessive saving necessarily fixed itself in capital goods.

Nor is this quite the end of Keynes' intellectual debts to other economists. Irving Fisher is the parent of the marginal efficiency of capital. And the multiplier – the gadget which has over the years attracted enormous attention – is the invention of Keynes' Cambridge associate R. F. Kahn. Keynes himself gladly acknowledged both of these predecessors.

Conclusion

Where does the argument come out? Should a judicious student vote for "revolution" or "continuity"? It cannot be denied that much of the Keynesian structure is anticipated, often in highly sophisticated form. It is equally accurate to say that Keynes' technique is Cambridge technique and that Cambridge technique after all is orthodox English economics. Thus from the most austere heights of economic doctrine, it is probably right to award victory to those who emphasize the Keynesian continuities with English and, secondarily, Scandinavian economics.

However, there is a still stronger case for the alternative proposition that Keynesian economics represent an important discontinuity in economic thinking. As an economic theorist, Keynes' radicalism was primarily in his choice of topics and variables. Keynes struck a major blow at orthodoxy by placing *employment* at the center of his macroeconomics and displacing price levels from their accustomed situation of honor. Perhaps he acted more dangerously still by his insistence upon the primacy of macroeconomics and the subordinate status of microeconomics.

These initiatives in turn depended upon the demolition of Say's Law,[1] the durable generalization which denied that "gluts" or involuntary unemployment could occur in competitive markets. Keynes' polemical assault stretched from Say's Law to his Cambridge associate and teacher A. C. Pigou's highly sophisticated adaptation of Say in his *Theory of Unemployment,* one of Keynes' favorite targets.

Economists now agree that Keynes treated Pigou harshly, even unfairly. Nevertheless, the lasting theoretical as well as the immediate practical significance of the *General Theory* is to be found in Keynes' destruction of this classical bogey and his demonstration that general glut and involuntary unemployment are perfectly explicable on theoretical grounds as the common positions of actual economic magnitudes. Keynes' demonstration is extraordinarily difficult to untangle. Although a portion of his exposition appears later in this volume, it is worth summarizing Keynes' position here. He started by defining the premises that underlay the "classical" proposition that in competitive labor and commodity markets, a wage reduction expanded employment and larger wage reductions expanded employment still more. In turn these theorems implied an even larger conclusion, that, aside from temporary, frictional pauses between jobs by workers, involuntary unemployment could not exist. At some wage rate – however low – full employment was always attainable.

The first "classical" wage theorem, then amounted to the statement, "the wage is equal to the marginal product of labor," or, in plainer English, the selling price of a worker's net output for the period covered by his wage. Keynes did not demur from this theorem. But he questioned a second theorem which he stated as follows: "The utility of the wage when a given volume of labour is employed is equal to the marginal disutility of that amount of employment." This

[1] In David Ricardo's early 19th-century formulation, Say's Law read like this: "No man produces but with a view to consume or sell, and he never sells but with an intention to purchase some other commodity. . . . By purchasing them, he necessarily becomes either the consumer of his own goods, or the purchaser and the consumer of the goods of some other person. . . . Productions are always bought by productions, or by services. . . ."

statement in turn can be translated into a number of propositions clearly tainted with Benthamite ancestry:

(1) Work is painful.

(2) Additional work becomes still more painful hour by hour.

(3) Wages please their recipients because they command objects and services which yield pleasures to their purchasers.

(4) But additional wages yield less pleasure, dollar by dollar, than their predecessors because they gratify tastes of diminishing intensity.

(5) Hence any worker will offer his services only as long as the pleasure he anticipates from his additional earnings exceeds the pain he incurs from his additional labor. In any actual market situation, he will cease to work just before the point at which additional pains match additional pleasures.

This extension of Bentham, the achievement of 19th and 20th century marginalists, also implies that an individual can increase his own employment by revising his computations of pleasure and pain so as to work more hours at existing wage rates, the same number at lower wage rates, or accept employment at a wage rate which he had previously deemed unacceptable. From this chain of reasoning came an important market judgment, nothing less than the conclusion that when actual unemployment characterized labor markets, then workers who were fully or partially unemployed could remedy their condition by accepting wage reductions. From this judgment flowed yet another generalization: a situation of general unemployment must be understood as the outcome of voluntary choices on the part of the unemployed.

It is probably just as well that ordinary citizens during the years of the Great Depression of the 1930's were spared expositions of this variety. Even the vulgarizations of this doctrine which filtered down to the general public scarcely enhanced the public's opinion of economics and economists. As far as anyone could see, the experts had not advanced beyond the austere advice of the English journal, *The Economist,* which in 1863 had these tender words to offer to unemployed cotton mill operatives:

> No man or woman has a right to ask or has reason to expect to be paid at the same rate for their labour, when there are 250,000 operatives out of work, as when all are fully employed. No man can expect that wages should be as high per day or per piece when trade is slack and losing, as when it is brisk and profitable. A lower rate of pay is the natural and inevitable result of the present state of the Lancashire labour market. . . . No operative who had refused work at *subsistence* wages ought to be held entitled to eleemosynary aid.

This was still the theory and in economics as in other subjects bad theory holds its ground until better theory displaces it, even in the face of overwhelming evidence that millions of the unemployed would gladly have accepted work at almost any rate above zero. Keynes' better theory – the judgment that unemployment was not after all the fault of the unemployed – is concealed in one of the more opaque definitions of economic theory:

> Men are involuntarily unemployed if, in the event of a small rise in the price of wage-goods relatively to the money wage, both the aggregate supply of labour willing to work for the current money-wage and the aggregate demand for it at that wage would be greater than the existing volume of employment.

Or, as a free translation might have it, "People must be out of jobs against their wills if, in the event of a rise in the cost of living and a resulting decline in real wages, employers seek to hire additional workers and these additional workers willingly allow themselves to be hired." Is it not only good sense to realize that if more men and women will gladly labor at *lower* real wages, even an economist must concede that they must have been unemployed against their own wishes when real wages were *higher*.

Thus it came to be that Keynes granted involuntary unemployment a theoretical license to exist. It is difficult to exaggerate the liberating effects of this reasoning. None too soon for economists, it resolved the contradiction between the evidence of their own eyes that unemployment was not the free choice of the unemployed, and a theory which commanded them to believe that mass unemployment was the consequence of individual reluctance to accept lower wages, trade union intransigence, business monopoly, unsound public finance, or all four put together. It is in this light that Keynes' break with his classical antecedents is sharpest and most important in both theory and practice. The Keynesian critics who argue that Keynes' doctrines of underemployment equilibrium depend on assumptions of wage and price rigidity, no doubt score important *theoretical* points against the Keynesian claims to generality. The practical importance of their achievement is small, for every advanced western society is characterized by institutional barriers against declining commodity prices and labor incomes. It is Keynes' triumph and his break with the past that his conclusions apply closely to economies we know about, not economies that economists have often preferred to write about.

KEYNES AND THE CLASSICS

PART ONE

THE CASE FOR THE KEYNESIAN REVOLUTION

INTRODUCTION

The first five items in this section are a battle cry. In Keynes' own language, they proclaim the maximum case for the proposition that the *General Theory of Employment, Interest and Money* amounts to a revolutionary break with the past history of economic theory in general, and Cambridge economics in particular. Thus Keynes starts with definitions of "classical" and "special" which make it easier for him as the argument proceeds to contrast Keynesian and classical doctrine, and general and special cases in a manner highly favorable to the Keynesian and the "general" and highly critical of the classical and the special.

As Keynes identifies the classical postulates, essentially of Alfred Marshall and A. C. Pigou, they center around Say's Law and the denial of the possibility of general involuntary unemployment. As the Introduction to this volume noted, Keynes' own rather difficult definition of involuntary unemployment emphasized both the possibility and the probability of its occurrence in real life. Hence the classical insistence that unemployment was either frictional or the consequence of a voluntary refusal to accept lower wages was wrong in theory and disastrous as a guide to economic policy. According to Keynes, workers cannot in most circumstances increase aggregate employment no matter how low a wage they accept.

Keynes is almost as ruthless in his treatment of the classical theory of interest. That theory had long insisted that the demand for savings was determined by the marginal productivity of capital and the supply of savings was governed by the time preferences of savers. The interest rate, according to this theory, served the role primarily of bringing into balance the demand and the supply of savings. The doctrine was always a useful ally of Say's Law, for if interest rates were low savers tended to save less and spend more on current consumption. If interest rates were high, they tended to furnish more funds for capital investment. By easy inference, the true believers might conclude that aggregate demand was always sufficient. All that savers, investors, and the interest rate among them did was to determine the allocation of productive effort between consumer goods and investment goods.

Demolition is one thing. Reconstruction is another. It was Keynes' strength that he provided new and ingenious substitutes for the theories which he assaulted. As it is possible to observe in the pages which follow, Keynes proposed to concentrate on macroeconomics instead of microeconomics. He offered as new constructions an aggregate demand function and an aggregate supply function. He buttressed this new approach with a theory of aggregate consumption, a liquidity preference doctrine of interest rate determination, and a transformation of economic policy in the direction of direct monetary and fiscal intervention.

These claims are not only Keynesian. The three remaining selections in this section in their fashion attest to the influence of Keynes. Professor Milton Friedman of the University of Chicago, long a critic of Keynesian economics, testifies nevertheless to the fruitful empirical research which the Keynesian consumption function has stimulated. Alvin Hansen, Professor Emeritus of Economics at Harvard University and long a leading American Keynesian, terms the consumption function the "great contribution" of the *General Theory*. Paul Sweezy, editor of the *Monthly Review* and a Marxist in economic orientation, all the same salutes Keynes' "penetrating analysis of the capitalist economy."

J. M. KEYNES

What is classical economics?*

"THE classical economists" was a name invented by Marx to cover Ricardo and James Mill and their *predecessors,* that is to say for the founders of the theory which culminated in the Ricardian economics. I have become accustomed, perhaps perpetrating a solecism, to include in "the classical school" the *followers* of Ricardo, those, that is to say, who adopted and perfected the theory of the Ricardian economics, including (for example) J. S. Mill, Marshall, Edgeworth and Prof. Pigou.

What is "general" about the *General Theory?*

I HAVE called this book the *General Theory of Employment, Interest and Money,* placing the emphasis on the prefix *general.* The object of such a title is to contrast the character of my arguments and conclusions with those of the *classical* theory of the subject, upon which I was brought up and which dominates the economic thought, both practical and theoretical, of the governing and academic classes of this generation, as it has for a hundred years past. I shall argue that the postulates of the classical theory are applicable to a special case only and not to the general case, the

* From the *General Theory of Employment, Interest and Money* by John Maynard Keynes. Reprinted by permission of Harcourt, Brace & World, Inc., pp. 3, 4–22.

situation which it assumes being a limiting point of the possible positions of equilibrium. Moreover, the characteristics of the special case assumed by the classical theory happen not to be those of the economic society in which we actually live, with the result that its teaching is misleading and disastrous if we attempt to apply it to the facts of experience.

J. M. KEYNES

What are the classical postulates? How does the new principle of effective demand contradict them?*

Most treatises on the theory of Value and Production are primarily concerned with the distribution of a *given* volume of employed resources between different uses and with the conditions which, assuming the employment of this quantity of resources, determine their relative rewards and the relative values of their products.[1]

* From the *General Theory of Employment, Interest and Money* by John Maynard Keynes. Reprinted by permission of Harcourt, Brace & World, Inc., pp. 4–22.

[1] This is in the Ricardian tradition. For Ricardo expressly repudiated any interest in the *amount* of the national dividend, as distinct from its distribution. In this he was assessing correctly the character of his own theory. But his successors, less clear-sighted, have used the classical theory in discussions concerning the causes of wealth. *Vide* Ricardo's letter to Malthus of October 9, 1820: "Political Economy you think is an enquiry into the nature and causes of wealth – I think it should be called an enquiry into the laws which determine the division of the produce of industry amongst the classes who concur in its formation. No law can be laid down respecting quantity, but a tolerably correct one can be laid down respecting proportions. Every day I am more satisfied that the former enquiry is vain and delusive, and the latter only the true objects of the science."

The question, also, of the volume of the *available* resources, in the sense of the size of the employable population, the extent of natural wealth and the accumulated capital equipment, has often been treated descriptively. But the pure theory of what determines the *actual employment* of the available resources has seldom been examined in great detail. To say that it has not been examined at all would, of course, be absurd. For every discussion concerning fluctuations of employment, of which there have been many, has been concerned with it. I mean, not that the topic has been overlooked, but that the fundamental theory underlying it has been deemed so simple and obvious that it has received, at the most, a bare mention.[2]

I

The classical theory of employment—supposedly simple and obvious—has been based, I think, on two fundamental postulates, though practically without discussion, namely:

I. *The wage is equal to the marginal product of labour.*

That is to say, the wage of an employed person is equal to the value which would be lost if employment were to be reduced by one unit (after deducting any other costs which this reduction of output would avoid); subject, however, to the qualification that the equality may be disturbed, in accordance with certain principles, if competition and markets are imperfect.

II. *The utility of the wage when a given volume of labour is employed is equal to the marginal disutility of that amount of employment.*

That is to say, the real wage of an employed person is that which is just sufficient (in the estimation of the employed persons themselves) to induce the volume of labour actually employed to be forthcoming; subject to the qualification that the equality for each individual unit of labour may be disturbed by combination between employable units analogous to the imperfections of competition which

[2] For example, Prof. Pigou in the *Economics of Welfare* (4th ed. p. 127) writes (my italics): "Throughout this discussion, except when the contrary is expressly stated, the fact that some resources are generally unemployed against the will of the owners is ignored. *This does not affect the substance of the argument,* while it simplifies its exposition." Thus, whilst Ricardo expressly disclaimed any attempt to deal with the amount of the national dividend as a whole, Prof. Pigou, in a book which is specifically directed to the problem of the national dividend, maintains that the same theory holds good when there is some involuntary unemployment as in the case of full employment.

qualify the first postulate. Disutility must be here understood to cover every kind of reason which might lead a man, or a body of men, to withhold their labour rather than accept a wage which had to them a utility below a certain minimum.

This postulate is compatible with what may be called "frictional" unemployment. For a realistic interpretation of it legitimately allows for various inexactnesses of adjustment which stand in the way of continuous full employment: for example, unemployment due to a temporary want of balance between the relative quantities of specialised resources as a result of miscalculation or intermittent demand; or to time-lags consequent on unforeseen changes; or to the fact that the change-over from one employment to another cannot be effected without a certain delay, so that there will always exist in a non-static society a proportion of resources unemployed "between jobs." In addition to "frictional" unemployment, the postulate is also compatible with "voluntary" unemployment due to the refusal or inability of a unit of labour, as a result of legislation or social practices or of combination for collective bargaining or of slow response to change or of mere human obstinacy, to accept a reward corresponding to the value of the product attributable to its marginal productivity. But these two categories of "frictional" unemployment and "voluntary" unemployment are comprehensive. The classical postulates do not admit of the possibility of the third category, which I shall define below as "involuntary" unemployment.

Subject to these qualifications, the volume of employed resources is duly determined, according to the classical theory, by the two postulates. The first gives us the demand schedule for employment, the second gives us the supply schedule; and the amount of employment is fixed at the point where the utility of the marginal product balances the disutility of the marginal employment.

It would follow from this that there are only four possible means of increasing employment:

(*a*) An improvement in organisation or in foresight which diminishes "frictional" unemployment;

(*b*) a decrease in the marginal disutility of labour, as expressed by the real wage for which additional labour is available, so as to diminish "voluntary" unemployment;

(*c*) an increase in the marginal physical productivity of labour in the wage-goods industries (to use Professor Pigou's convenient term for goods upon the price of which the utility of the money-wage depends);

or (*d*) an increase in the price of non-wage-goods compared with the price of wage-goods, associated with a shift in the expenditure of non-wage-earners from wage-goods to non-wage-goods.

This, to the best of my understanding, is the substance of Professor Pigou's *Theory of Unemployment* – the only detailed account of the classical theory of employment which exists.

II

Is it true that the above categories are comprehensive in view of the fact that the population generally is seldom doing as much work as it would like to do on the basis of the current wage? For, admittedly, more labour would, as a rule, be forthcoming at the existing money-wage if it were demanded.[3] The classical school reconcile this phenomenon with their second postulate by arguing that, while the demand for labour at the existing money-wage may be satisfied before everyone willing to work at this wage is employed, this situation is due to an open or tacit agreement amongst workers not to work for less, and that if labour as a whole would agree to a reduction of money-wages more employment would be forthcoming. If this is the case, such unemployment, though apparently involuntary, is not strictly so, and ought to be included under the above category of "voluntary" unemployment due to the effects of collective bargaining, etc.

This calls for two observations, the first of which relates to the actual attitude of workers towards real wages and money-wages respectively and is not theoretically fundamental, but the second of which is fundamental.

Let us assume, for the moment, that labour is not prepared to work for a lower money-wage and that a reduction in the existing level of money-wages would lead, through strikes or otherwise, to a withdrawal from the labour market of labour which is now employed. Does it follow from this that the existing level of real wages accurately measures the marginal disutility of labour? Not necessarily. For, although a reduction in the existing money-wage would lead to a withdrawal of labour, it does not follow that a fall in the value of the existing money-wage in terms of wage-goods would do so, if it were due to a rise in the price of the latter. In other words, it may be the case that within a certain range the demand of labour is for a minimum money-wage and not for a minimum real wage. The classical school have tacitly assumed that this would involve no significant change in their theory. But this is not so. For if the supply of labour

[3] *Cf.* the quotation from Prof. Pigou above, p. 5, footnote.

is not a function of real wages as its sole variable, their argument breaks down entirely and leaves the question of what the actual employment will be quite indeterminate. They do not seem to have realised that, unless the supply of labour is a function of real wages alone, their supply curve for labour will shift bodily with every movement of prices. Thus their method is tied up with their very special assumptions, and cannot be adapted to deal with the more general case.

Now ordinary experience tells us, beyond doubt, that a situation where labour stipulates (within limits) for a money-wage rather than a real wage, so far from being a mere possibility, is the normal case. Whilst workers will usually resist a reduction of money-wages, it is not their practice to withdraw their labour whenever there is a rise in the price of wage-goods. It is sometimes said that it would be illogical for labour to resist a reduction of money-wages but not to resist a reduction of real wages. For reasons given below (p. 11), this might not be so illogical as it appears at first; and, as we shall see later, fortunately so. But, whether logical or illogical, experience shows that this is how labour in fact behaves.

Moreover, the contention that the unemployment which characterises a depression is due to a refusal by labour to accept a reduction of money-wages is not clearly supported by the facts. It is not very plausible to assert that unemployment in the United States in 1932 was due either to labour obstinately refusing to accept a reduction of money-wages or to its obstinately demanding a real wage beyond what the productivity of the economic machine was capable of furnishing. Wide variations are experienced in the volume of employment without any apparent change either in the minimum real demands of labour or in its productivity. Labour is not more truculent in the depression than in the boom—far from it. Nor is its physical productivity less. These facts from experience are a *prima facie* ground for questioning the adequacy of the classical analysis.

It would be interesting to see the results of a statistical enquiry into the actual relationship between changes in money-wages and changes in real wages. In the case of a change peculiar to a particular industry one would expect the change in real wages to be in the same direction as the change in money-wages. But in the case of changes in the general level of wages, it will be found, I think, that the change in real wages associated with a change in money-wages, so far from being usually in the same direction, is almost always in the opposite direction. When money-wages are rising, that is to say, it will be found that real wages are falling; and when money-wages are falling, real wages are rising. This is because, in the short period, falling money-wages and rising real wages are each, for independent reasons, likely to accompany decreasing employment; labour being readier to accept wage-cuts when employment is falling off, yet real wages inevitably rising in the same circumstances on account of the increasing marginal return to a given capital equipment when output is diminished.

If, indeed, it were true that the existing real wage is a minimum below which more labour than is now employed will not be forthcoming in any circumstances, involuntary unemployment, apart from frictional unemployment, would be non-existent. But to suppose that this is invariably the case would be absurd. For more labour than is at present employed is usually available at the existing money-wage, even though the price of wage-goods is rising and, consequently, the real wage falling. If this is true, the wage-goods equivalent of the existing money-wage is not an accurate indication of the marginal disutility of labour, and the second postulate does not hold good.

But there is a more fundamental objection. The second postulate flows from the idea that the real wages of labour depend on the wage bargains which labour makes with the entrepreneurs. It is admitted, of course, that the bargains are actually made in terms of money, and even that the real wages acceptable to labour are not altogether independent of what the corresponding money-wage happens to be. Nevertheless it is the money-wage thus arrived at which is held to determine the real wage. Thus the classical theory assumes that it is always open to labour to reduce its real wage by accepting a reduction in its money-wage. The postulate that there is a tendency for the real wage to come to equality with the marginal disutility of labour clearly presumes that labour itself is in a position to decide the real wage for which it works, though not the quantity of employment forthcoming at this wage.

The traditional theory maintains, in short, *that the wage bargains between the entrepreneurs and the workers determine the real wage;* so that, assuming free competition amongst employers and no restrictive combination amongst workers, the latter can, if they wish, bring their real wages into conformity with the marginal disutility of the amount of employment offered by the employers at that wage. If this is not true, then there is no longer any reason to expect a tendency towards equality between the real wage and the marginal disutility of labour.

The classical conclusions are intended, it must be remembered, to apply to the whole body of labour and do not mean merely that a single individual can get employment by accepting a cut in money-wages which his fellows refuse. They are supposed to be equally applicable to a closed system as to an open system, and are not dependent on the characteristics of an open system or on the effects of a reduction of money-wages in a single country on its foreign trade, which lie, of course, entirely outside the field of this discussion. Nor are they based on indirect effects due to a lower wages-bill in terms of money having certain reactions on the banking system and the state of credit, effects which we shall examine in detail in Chapter 19. They are based on the belief that in a closed system a reduction in the general level of money-wages will be accompanied, at any rate in the short period and subject only to minor qualifications, by some, though not always a proportionate, reduction in real wages.

Now the assumption that the general level of real wages depends on the money-wage bargains between the employers and the workers is not obviously true. Indeed it is strange that so little attempt should have been made to prove or to refute it. For it is far from being consistent with the general tenor of the classical theory, which has taught us to believe that prices are governed by marginal prime cost in terms of money and that money-wages largely govern marginal prime cost. Thus if money-wages change, one would have expected the classical school to argue that prices would change in almost the same proportion, leaving the real wage and the level of unemployment practically the same as before, any small gain or loss to labour being at the expense or profit of other elements of marginal cost which have been left unaltered. They seem, however, to have been diverted from this line of thought, partly by the settled conviction that labour is in a position to determine its own real wage and partly, perhaps, by preoccupation with the idea that prices depend on the quantity of money. And the belief in the proposition that labour is always in a position to determine its own real wage, once adopted, has been maintained by its being confused with the proposition that labour is always in a position to determine what real wage shall correspond to *full* employment, *i.e.* the *maximum* quantity of employment which is compatible with a given real wage.

To sum up: there are two objections to the second postulate of the classical theory. The first relates to the actual behaviour of labour. A fall in real wages due to a rise in prices, with money-wages unaltered, does not, as a rule, cause the supply of available labour on offer at the current wage to fall below the amount actually employed prior to the rise of prices. To suppose that it does is to suppose that all those who are now unemployed though willing to work at the current wage will withdraw the offer of their labour in the event of even a small rise in the cost of living. Yet this strange supposition apparently underlies Professor Pigou's *Theory of Unemployment*, and it is what all members of the orthodox school are tacitly assuming.

But the other, more fundamental, objection, which we shall develop in the ensuing chapters, flows from our disputing the assumption that the general level of real wages is directly determined by the character of the wage bargain. In assuming that the wage bargain determines the real wage the classical school have slipt in an illicit assumption. For there may be *no* method available to labour as a whole whereby it can bring the wage-goods equivalent of the general level of money-wages into conformity with the marginal disutility of the current volume of employment. There may exist no expedient by which labour as a whole can reduce its *real* wage to a given figure by making revised *money* bargains with the entrepreneurs. This will be our contention. We shall endeavour to show that primarily it is certain other forces which determine the general level of real wages. The attempt to elucidate this problem will be one of our main themes. We shall argue that there has been a fundamental misunderstanding of how in this respect the economy in which we live actually works.

III

Though the struggle over money-wages between individuals and groups is often believed to determine the general level of real wages, it is, in fact, concerned with a different object. Since there is imperfect mobility of labour, and wages do not tend to an exact equality of net advantage in different occupations, any individual or group of individuals, who consent to a reduction of money-wages relatively to others, will suffer a *relative* reduction in real wages, which is a sufficient justification for them to resist it. On the other hand it would be impracticable to resist every reduction of real wages, due to a change in the purchasing-power of money which affects all workers alike; and in fact reductions of real wages arising in this way are not, as a rule, resisted unless they proceed to an extreme degree. Moreover, a resistance to reductions in money-wages applying to particular industries does not raise the same insuperable bar to an increase in aggregate employment which would result from a similar resistance to every reduction in real wages.

In other words, the struggle about money-wages primarily affects the *distribution* of the aggregate real wage between different labour-groups, and not its average amount per unit of employment, which depends, as we shall see, on a different set of forces. The effect of combination on the part of a group of workers is to protect their *relative* real wage. The *general* level of real wages depends on the other forces of the economic system.

Thus it is fortunate that the workers, though unconsciously, are instinctively more reasonable economists than the classical school, inasmuch as they resist reductions of money-wages, which are seldom or never of an all-round character, even though the existing real equivalent of these wages exceeds the marginal disutility of the existing employment; whereas they do not resist reductions of real wages, which are associated with increases in aggregate employment and leave relative money-wages unchanged, unless the reduction proceeds so far as to threaten a reduction of the real wage below the marginal disutility of the existing volume of employment. Every trade union will put up some resistance to a cut in money-wages, however small. But since no trade union would dream of striking on every occasion of a rise in the cost of living, they do not raise the obstacle to any increase in aggregate employment which is attributed to them by the classical school.

IV

We must now define the third category of unemployment, namely "involuntary" unemployment in the strict sense, the possibility of which the classical theory does not admit.

Clearly we do not mean by "involuntary" unemployment the mere existence of an unexhausted capacity to work. An eight-hour day does not constitute unemployment because it is not beyond human capacity to work ten hours. Nor should we regard as "involuntary" unemployment the withdrawal of their labour by a body of workers because they do not choose to work for less than a certain real reward. Furthermore, it will be convenient to exclude "frictional" unemployment from our definition of "involuntary" unemployment. My definition is, therefore, as follows: *Men are involuntarily unemployed if, in the event of a small rise in the price of wage-goods relatively to the money-wage, both the aggregate supply of labour willing to work for the current money-wage and the aggregate demand for it at that wage would be greater than the existing volume of employment.* An alternative definition, which amounts, however, to the same thing, will be given in the next chapter (p. 19 below).

It follows from this definition that the equality of the real wage to the marginal disutility of employment presupposed by the second postulate, realistically interpreted, corresponds to the absence of "involuntary" unemployment. This state of affairs we shall describe as "full" employment, both "frictional" and "voluntary" unemployment being consistent with "full" employment thus defined. This fits in, we shall find, with other characteristics of the classical theory, which is best regarded as a theory of distribution in conditions of full employment. So long as the classical postulates hold good, unemployment, which is in the above sense involuntary, cannot occur. Apparent unemployment must, therefore, be the result either of temporary loss of work of the "between jobs" type or of intermittent demand for highly specialised resources or of the effect of a trade union "closed shop" on the employment of free labour. Thus writers in the classical tradition, overlooking the special assumption underlying their theory, have been driven inevitably to the conclusion, perfectly logical on their assumption, that apparent unemployment (apart from the admitted exceptions) must be due at bottom to a refusal by the unemployed factors to accept a reward which corresponds to their marginal productivity. A classical economist may sympathise with labour in refusing to accept a cut in its money-wage, and he will admit that it may not be wise to make it to meet conditions which are temporary; but scientific integrity forces him to declare that this refusal is, nevertheless, at the bottom of the trouble.

Obviously, however, if the classical theory is only applicable to the case of full employment, it is fallacious to apply it to the problems of involuntary unemployment—if there be such a thing (and who will deny it?). The classical theorists resemble Euclidean geometers in a non-Euclidean world who, discovering that in experience straight lines apparently parallel often meet, rebuke the lines for not keeping straight—as the only remedy for the unfortunate collisions which are occurring. Yet, in truth, there is no remedy except to throw over the axiom of parallels and to work out a non-Euclidean geometry. Something similar is required to-day in economics. We need to throw over the second postulate of the classical doctrine and to work out the behaviour of a system in which involuntary unemployment in the strict sense is possible.

V

In emphasising our point of departure from the classical system, we must not overlook an important point of agreement. For we shall maintain the first postulate as heretofore, subject only to the same qualifications as in the classical theory; and we must pause, for a moment, to consider what this involves.

It means that, with a given organisation, equipment and technique, real wages and the volume of output (and hence of employment) are uniquely correlated, so that, in general, an increase in employment can only occur to the accompaniment of a decline in the rate of real wages. Thus I am not disputing this vital fact which the classical economists have (rightly) asserted as indefeasible. In a given state of organisation, equipment and technique, the real wage earned by a unit of labour has a unique (inverse) correlation with the volume of employment. Thus *if* employment increases, then, in the short period, the reward per unit of labour in terms of wage-goods must, in general, decline and profits increase.[4] This is simply the obverse of the familiar proposition that industry is normally working subject to decreasing returns in the short period during which equipment etc. is assumed to be constant; so that the marginal product in the wage-good industries (which governs real wages) necessarily diminishes as employment is increased. So long, indeed, as this proposition holds, *any* means of increasing employment must lead at the same time to a diminution of the marginal product and hence of the rate of wages measured in terms of this product.

But when we have thrown over the second postulate, a decline in employment, although necessarily associated with labour's *receiving* a wage equal in value to a larger quantity of wage-goods, is not necessarily due to labour's *demanding* a larger quantity of wage-goods; and a willingness on the part of labour to accept lower money-wages is not necessarily a remedy for unemployment. The Theory of Wages in relation to employment, to which we are here leading up, cannot be fully elucidated, however, until Chapter 19 and its appendix have been reached.

VI

From the time of Say and Ricardo the classical economists have taught that supply creates its own demand; — meaning by this in some significant, but not clearly defined, sense that the whole of the costs of production must necessarily be spent in the aggregate, directly or indirectly, on purchasing the product.

[4] The argument runs as follows: n men are employed, the nth man adds a bushel a day to the harvest, and wages have a buying power of a bushel a day. The $n + 1$th man, however, would only add .9 bushel a day, and employment cannot, therefore, rise to $n + 1$ men unless the price of corn rises relatively to wages until daily wages have a buying power of .9 bushel. Aggregate wages would then amount to $\frac{9}{10}(n + 1)$ bushels as compared with n bushels previously. Thus the employment of an additional man will, if it occurs, necessarily involve a transfer of income from those previously in work to the entrepreneurs.

In J. S. Mill's *Principles of Political Economy* the doctrine is expressly set forth:

What constitutes the means of payment for commodities is simply commodities. Each person's means of paying for the productions of other people consist of those which he himself possesses. All sellers are inevitably, and by the meaning of the word, buyers. Could we suddenly double the productive powers of the country, we should double the supply of commodities in every market; but we should, by the same stroke, double the purchasing power. Everybody would bring a double demand as well as supply; everybody would be able to buy twice as much, because every one would have twice as much to offer in exchange.

As a corollary of the same doctrine, it has been supposed that any individual act of abstaining from consumption necessarily leads to, and amounts to the same thing as, causing the labour and commodities thus released from supplying consumption to be invested in the production of capital wealth. The following passage from Marshall's *Pure Theory of Domestic Values* illustrates the traditional approach:

The whole of a man's income is expended in the purchase of services and of commodities. It is indeed commonly said that a man spends some portion of his income and saves another. But it is a familiar economic axiom that a man purchases labour and commodities with that portion of his income which he saves just as much as he does with that he is said to spend. He is said to spend when he seeks to obtain present enjoyment from the services and commodities which he purchases. He is said to save when he causes the labour and the commodities which he purchases to be devoted to the production of wealth from which he expects to derive the means of enjoyment in the future.

It is true that it would not be easy to quote comparable passages from Marshall's later work[5] or from Edgeworth or Professor Pigou. The doctrine is never stated to-day in this crude form. Nevertheless it still underlies the whole classical theory, which would collapse without it. Contemporary economists, who might hesitate to agree with Mill, do not hesitate to accept conclusions which require Mill's doc-

[5] Mr. J. A. Hobson, after quoting in his *Physiology of Industry* (p. 102) the above passage from Mill, points out that Marshall commented as follows on this passage as early as his *Economics of Industry*, p. 154. "But though men have the power to purchase, they may not choose to use it." "But," Mr. Hobson continues, "he fails to grasp the critical importance of this fact, and appears to limit its action to periods of 'crisis.'" This has remained fair comment, I think, in the light of Marshall's later work.

trine as their premiss. The conviction, which runs, for example, through almost all Professor Pigou's work, that money makes no real difference except frictionally and that the theory of production and employment can be worked out (like Mill's) as being based on "real" exchanges with money introduced perfunctorily in a later chapter, is the modern version of the classical tradition. Contemporary thought is still deeply steeped in the notion that if people do not spend their money in one way they will spend it in another.[6] Post-war economists seldom, indeed, succeed in maintaining this standpoint *consistently*; for their thought to-day is too much permeated with the contrary tendency and with facts of experience too obviously inconsistent with their former view.[7] But they have not drawn sufficiently far-reaching consequences; and have not revised their fundamental theory.

In the first instance, these conclusions may have been applied to the kind of economy in which we actually live by false analogy from some kind of non-exchange Robinson Crusoe economy, in which the income which individuals consume or retain as a result of their productive activity is, actually and exclusively, the output *in specie* of that activity. But, apart from this, the conclusion that the *costs* of output are always covered in the aggregate by the sale-proceeds resulting from demand, has great plausibility, because it is difficult to distinguish it from another, similar-looking proposition which is indubitable, namely that the income derived in the aggregate by all the elements in the community concerned in a productive activity necessarily has a value exactly equal to the *value* of the output.

Similarly it is natural to suppose that the act of an individual, by which he enriches himself without apparently taking anything from anyone else, must also enrich the community as a whole; so that (as in the passage just quoted from Marshall) an act of individual saving inevitably leads to a parallel act of investment. For, once more, it is indubitable that the sum of the net increments of the wealth of

[6] *Cf.* Alfred and Mary Marshall, *Economics of Industry*, p. 17: "It is not good for trade to have dresses made of material which wears out quickly. For if people did not spend their means on buying new dresses they would spend them on giving employment to labour in some other way." The reader will notice that I am again quoting from the earlier Marshall. The Marshall of the *Principles* had become sufficiently doubtful to be very cautious and evasive. But the old ideas were never repudiated or rooted out of the basic assumptions of his thought.

[7] It is the distinction of Prof. Robbins that he, almost alone, continues to maintain a consistent scheme of thought, his practical recommendations belonging to the same system as his theory.

individuals must be exactly equal to the aggregate net increment of the wealth of the community.

Those who think in this way are deceived, nevertheless, by an optical illusion, which makes two essentially different activities appear to be the same. They are fallaciously supposing that there is a nexus which unites decisions to abstain from present consumption with decisions to provide for future consumption; whereas the motives which determine the latter are not linked in any simple way with the motives which determine the former.

It is, then, the assumption of equality between the demand price of output as a whole and its supply price which is to be regarded as the classical theory's "axiom of parallels." Granted this, all the rest follows – the social advantages of private and national thrift, the traditional attitude towards the rate of interest, the classical theory of unemployment, the quantity theory of money, the unqualified advantages of *laissez-faire* in respect of foreign trade and much else which we shall have to question.

VII

At different points in this chapter we have made the classical theory to depend in succession on the assumptions:

(1) that the real wage is equal to the marginal disutility of the existing employment;
(2) that there is no such thing as involuntary unemployment in the strict sense;
(3) that supply creates its own demand in the sense that the aggregate demand price is equal to the aggregate supply price for all levels of output and employment.

These three assumptions, however, all amount to the same thing in the sense that they all stand and fall together, any one of them logically involving the other two.

J. M. KEYNES

What is aggregate demand? What is aggregate supply?*

I

We need, to start with, a few terms which will be defined precisely later. In a given state of technique, resources and costs, the employment of a given volume of labour by an entrepreneur involves him in two kinds of expense: first of all, the amounts which he pays out to the factors of production (exclusive of other entrepreneurs) for their current services, which we shall call the *factor cost* of the employment in question; and secondly, the amounts which he pays out to other entrepreneurs for what he has to purchase from them together with the sacrifice which he incurs by employing the equipment instead of leaving it idle, which we shall call the *user cost* of the employment in question. The excess of the value of the resulting output over the sum of its factor cost and its user cost is the profit or, as we shall call it, the *income* of the entrepreneur. The factor cost is, of course, the same thing, looked at from the point of view of the entrepreneur, as what the factors of production regard as their income. Thus the factor cost and the entrepreneur's profit make up, between them, what we shall define as the *total income* resulting from the employment given by the entrepreneur. The entrepreneur's profit thus defined is, as it should be, the quantity which he endeavours to maximise when he is deciding what amount of employment to offer. It is sometimes convenient, when we are looking at it from the entrepreneur's standpoint, to call the aggregate income (*i.e.* factor cost *plus* profit) resulting from a given amount of employment the *proceeds* of that employment. On the other hand, the aggregate supply price of the output of a given amount of employment is the expectation of proceeds which will just make it worth the while of the entrepreneurs to give that employment.

* From the *General Theory of Employment, Interest and Money* by John Maynard Keynes. Reprinted by permission of Harcourt, Brace & World, Inc., pp. 23–26.

It follows that in a given situation of technique, resources and factor cost per unit of employment, the amount of employment, both in each individual firm and industry and in the aggregate, depends on the amount of the proceeds which the entrepreneurs expect to receive from the corresponding output. For entrepreneurs will endeavour to fix the amount of employment at the level which they expect to maximise the excess of the proceeds over the factor cost.

Let Z be the aggregate supply price of the output from employing N men, the relationship between Z and N being written $Z = \phi(N)$, which can be called the *Aggregate Supply Function*. Similarly, let D be the proceeds which entrepreneurs expect to receive from the employment of N men, the relationship between D and N being written $D = f(N)$, which can be called the *Aggregate Demand Function*.

Now if for a given value of N the expected proceeds are greater than the aggregate supply price, *i.e.* if D is greater than Z, there will be an incentive to entrepreneurs to increase employment beyond N and, if necessary, to raise costs by competing with one another for the factors of production, up to the value of N for which Z has become equal to D. Thus the volume of employment is given by the point of intersection between the aggregate demand function and the aggregate supply function; for it is at this point that the entrepreneurs' expectation of profits will be maximised. The value of D at the point of the aggregate demand function, where it is intersected by the aggregate supply function, will be called *the effective demand*. Since this is the substance of the General Theory of Employment, which it will be our object to expound, the succeeding chapters will be largely occupied with examining the various factors upon which these two functions depend.

The classical doctrine, on the other hand, which used to be expressed categorically in the statement that "Supply creates its own Demand" and continues to underlie all orthodox economic theory, involves a special assumption as to the relationship between these two functions. For "Supply creates its own Demand" must mean that $f(N)$ and $\phi(N)$ are equal for *all* values of N, *i.e.* for all levels of output and employment; and that when there is an increase in $Z(= \phi(N))$ corresponding to an increase in N, $D(= f(N))$ necessarily increases by the same amount as Z. The classical theory assumes, in other words, that the aggregate demand price (or proceeds) always accommodates itself to the aggregate supply price; so that, whatever the value of N may be, the proceeds D assume a value equal to the aggregate supply price Z which corresponds to N. That is to say, effective demand, instead of having a unique equilibrium value, is an infinite range of values all equally admissible; and the amount of employment is indeterminate except in so far as the marginal disutility of labour sets an upper limit.

If this were true, competition between entrepreneurs would always lead to an expansion of employment up to the point at which the supply of output as a whole ceases to be elastic, *i.e.* where a further increase in the value of the effective demand will no longer be accompanied by any increase in output. Evidently this amounts to the same thing as full employment. In the previous chapter we have given a definition of full employment in terms of the behaviour of labour. An alternative, though equivalent, criterion is that at which we have now arrived, namely a situation in which aggregate employment is inelastic in response to an increase in the effective demand for its output. Thus Say's Law, that the aggregate demand price of output as a whole is equal to its aggregate supply price for all volumes of output, is equivalent to the proposition that there is no obstacle to full employment. If, however, this is not the true law relating the aggregate demand and supply functions, there is a vitally important chapter of economic theory which remains to be written and without which all discussions concerning the volume of aggregate employment are futile.

J. M. KEYNES

How does the theory fit together?*

A BRIEF summary of the theory of employment to be worked out in the course of the following chapters may, perhaps, help the reader at this stage, even though it may not be fully intelligible.

* From the *General Theory of Employment, Interest and Money* by John Maynard Keynes. Reprinted by permission of Harcourt, Brace & World, Inc., pp. 27–34.

The terms involved will be more carefully defined in due course. In this summary we shall assume that the money-wage and other factor costs are constant per unit of labour employed. But this simplification, with which we shall dispense later, is introduced solely to facilitate the exposition. The essential character of the argument is precisely the same whether or not money-wages, etc., are liable to change.

The outline of our theory can be expressed as follows. When employment increases, aggregate real income is increased. The psychology of the community is such that when aggregate real income is increased aggregate consumption is increased, but not by so much as income. Hence employers would make a loss if the whole of the increased employment were to be devoted to satisfying the increased demand for immediate consumption. Thus, to justify any given amount of employment there must be an amount of current investment sufficient to absorb the excess of total output over what the community chooses to consume when employment is at the given level. For unless there is this amount of investment, the receipts of the entrepreneurs will be less than is required to induce them to offer the given amount of employment. It follows, therefore, that, given what we shall call the community's propensity to consume, the equilibrium level of employment, *i.e.* the level at which there is no inducement to employers as a whole either to expand or to contract employment, will depend on the amount of current investment. The amount of current investment will depend, in turn, on what we shall call the inducement to invest; and the inducement to invest will be found to depend on the relation between the schedule of the marginal efficiency of capital and the complex of rates of interest on loans of various maturities and risks.

Thus, given the propensity to consume and the rate of new investment, there will be only one level of employment consistent with equilibrium; since any other level will lead to inequality between the aggregate supply price of output as a whole and its aggregate demand price. This level cannot be *greater* than full employment, *i.e.* the real wage cannot be less than the marginal disutility of labour. But there is no reason in general for expecting it to be *equal* to full employment. The effective demand associated with full employment is a special case, only realised when the propensity to consume and the inducement to invest stand in a particular relationship to one another. This particular relationship, which corresponds to the assumptions of the classical theory, is in a sense an optimum relationship. But it can only exist when, by accident or design, current investment provides an amount of demand just equal to the excess of the aggregate supply price of the output resulting from full employment over what the community will choose to spend on consumption when it is fully employed.

This theory can be summed up in the following propositions:

(1) In a given situation of technique, resources and costs, income (both money-income and real income) depends on the volume of employment N.

(2) The relationship between the community's income and what it can be expected to spend on consumption, designated by D_1, will depend on the psychological characteristic of the community, which we shall call its *propensity to consume*. That is to say, consumption will depend on the level of aggregate income and, therefore, on the level of employment N, except when there is some change in the propensity to consume.

(3) The amount of labour N which the entrepreneurs decide to employ depends on the sum (D) of *two* quantities, namely D_1, the amount which the community is expected to spend on consumption, and D_2, the amount which it is expected to devote to new investment. D is what we have called above the *effective demand*.

(4) Since $D_1 + D_2 = D = \phi(N)$, where ϕ is the aggregate supply function, and since, as we have seen in (2) above, D_1 is a function of N, which we may write $\chi(N)$, depending on the propensity to consume, it follows that $\phi(N) - \chi(N) = D_2$.

(5) Hence the volume of employment in equilibrium depends on (i) the aggregate supply function, ϕ, (ii) the propensity to consume, χ, and (iii) the volume of investment, D_2. This is the essence of the General Theory of Employment.

(6) For every value of N there is a corresponding marginal productivity of labour in the wage goods industries; and it is this which determines the real wage. (5) is, therefore, subject to the condition that N cannot *exceed* the value which reduces the real wage to equality with the marginal disutility of labour. This means that not all changes in D are compatible with our temporary assumption that money-wages are constant. Thus it will be essential to a full statement of our theory to dispense with this assumption.

(7) On the classical theory, according to which $D = \phi(N)$ for *all* values of N, the volume of employment is in neutral equilibrium for all values of N less than its maximum value; so that the forces of competition between entrepreneurs may be expected to push it to this maximum value. Only at this point, on the classical theory, can there be stable equilibrium.

(8) *When employment increases,* D_1 *will increase, but not by so*

much as D; since when our income increases our consumption increases also, but not by so much. The key to our practical problem is to be found in this psychological law. For it follows from this that the greater the volume of employment the greater will be the gap between the aggregate supply price (Z) of the corresponding output and the sum (D_1) which the entrepreneurs can expect to get back out of the expenditure of consumers. Hence, if there is no change in the propensity to consume, employment cannot increase, unless at the same time D_2 is increasing so as to fill the increasing gap between Z and D_1. Thus – except on the special assumptions of the classical theory according to which there is some force in operation which, when employment increases, always causes D_2 to increase sufficiently to fill the widening gap between Z and D_1 – the economic system may find itself in stable equilibrium with N at a level below full employment, namely at the level given by the intersection of the aggregate demand function with the aggregate supply function.

Thus the volume of employment is not determined by the marginal disutility of labour measured in terms of real wages, except in so far as the supply of labour available at a given real wage sets a *maximum* level to employment. The propensity to consume and the rate of new investment determine between them the volume of employment, and the volume of employment is uniquely related to a given level of real wages – not the other way round. If the propensity to consume and the rate of new investment result in a deficient effective demand, the actual level of employment will fall short of the supply of labour potentially available at the existing real wage, and the equilibrium real wage will be *greater* than the marginal disutility of the equilibrium level of employment.

This analysis supplies us with an explanation of the paradox of poverty in the midst of plenty. For the mere existence of an insufficiency of effective demand may, and often will, bring the increase of employment to a standstill *before* a level of full employment has been reached. The insufficiency of effective demand will inhibit the process of production in spite of the fact that the marginal product of labour still exceeds in value the marginal disutility of employment.

Moreover the richer the community, the wider will tend to be the gap between its actual and its potential production; and therefore the more obvious and outrageous the defects of the economic system. For a poor community will be prone to consume by far the greater part of its output, so that a very modest measure of investment will be sufficient to provide full employment; whereas a wealthy community will have to discover much ampler opportunities for investment if the saving propensities of its wealthier members are to be compatible with the employment of its poorer members. If in a potentially wealthy community the inducement to invest is weak, then, in spite of its potential wealth, the working of the principle of effective demand will compel it to reduce its actual output, until, in spite of its potential wealth, it has become so poor that its surplus over its consumption is sufficiently diminished to correspond to the weakness of the inducement to invest.

But worse still. Not only is the marginal propensity to consume weaker in a wealthy community, but, owing to its accumulation of capital being already larger, the opportunities for further investment are less attractive unless the rate of interest falls at a sufficiently rapid rate; which brings us to the theory of the rate of interest and to the reasons why it does not automatically fall to the appropriate level, which will occupy Book IV.

Thus the analysis of the Propensity to Consume, the definition of the Marginal Efficiency of Capital and the theory of the Rate of Interest are the three main gaps in our existing knowledge which it will be necessary to fill. When this has been accomplished, we shall find that the Theory of Prices falls into its proper place as a matter which is subsidiary to our general theory. We shall discover, however, that Money plays an essential part in our theory of the Rate of Interest; and we shall attempt to disentangle the peculiar characteristics of Money which distinguish it from other things.

III

The idea that we can safely neglect the aggregate demand function is fundamental to the Ricardian economics, which underlie what we have been taught for more than a century. Malthus, indeed, had vehemently opposed Ricardo's doctrine that it was impossible for effective demand to be deficient; but vainly. For, since Malthus was unable to explain clearly (apart from an appeal to the facts of common observation) how and why effective demand could be deficient or excessive, he failed to furnish an alternative construction; and Ricardo conquered England as completely as the Holy Inquisition conquered Spain. Not only was his theory accepted by the city, by statesmen and by the academic world, but controversy ceased; the other point of view completely disappeared; it ceased to be discussed. The great puzzle of Effective Demand with which Malthus had wrestled vanished from economic literature. You will not find it mentioned even once in the whole works of Marshall, Edgeworth and Professor Pigou, from whose hands the classical theory has received its most mature embodiment. It could only live on furtively, below the surface, in the underworlds of Karl Marx, Silvio Gesell or Major Douglas.

The completeness of the Ricardian victory is something of a curiosity and a mystery. It must have been due to a complex of suitabilities in the doctrine to the environment into which it was projected. That it reached conclusions quite different from what the ordinary uninstructed person would expect, added, I suppose, to its intellectual prestige. That its teaching, translated into practice, was austere and often unpalatable, lent it virtue. That it was adapted to carry a vast and consistent logical superstructure, gave it beauty. That it could explain much social injustice and apparent cruelty as an inevitable incident in the scheme of progress, and the attempt to change such things as likely on the whole to do more harm than good, commended it to authority. That it afforded a measure of justification to the free activities of the individual capitalist, attracted to it the support of the dominant social force behind authority.

But although the doctrine itself has remained unquestioned by orthodox economists up to a late date, its signal failure for purposes of scientific prediction has greatly impaired, in the course of time, the prestige of its practitioners. For professional economists, after Malthus, were apparently unmoved by the lack of correspondence between the results of their theory and the facts of observation; – a discrepancy which the ordinary man has not failed to observe, with the result of his growing unwillingness to accord to economists that measure of respect which he gives to other groups of scientists whose theoretical results are confirmed by observation when they are applied to the facts.

The celebrated *optimism* of traditional economic theory, which has led to economists being looked upon as Candides, who, having left this world for the cultivation of their gardens, teach that all is for the best in the best of all possible worlds provided we will let well alone, is also to be traced, I think, to their having neglected to take account of the drag on prosperity which can be exercised by an insufficiency of effective demand. For there would obviously be a natural tendency towards the optimum employment of resources in a Society which was functioning after the manner of the classical postulates. It may well be that the classical theory represents the way in which we should like our Economy to behave. But to assume that it actually does so is to assume our difficulties away.

MILTON FRIEDMAN

How has the *General Theory* stimulated economic research?*

THE relation between aggregate consumption or aggregate savings and aggregate income, generally termed the consumption function, has occupied a major role in economic thinking ever since Keynes made it a keystone of his theoretical structure in *The General Theory*. Keynes took it for granted that current consumption expenditure is a highly dependable and stable function of current income—that "the amount of aggregate consumption mainly depends on the amount of aggregate income (both measured in terms of wage units)." He termed it a "fundamental psychological rule of any modern community that, when its real income is increased, it will not increase its consumption by an equal *absolute* amount," and stated somewhat less definitely that "as a rule, . . . a greater *proportion* of income . . . (is) saved as real income increases."[1]

Theoretical interest stimulated empirical work. Numerical consumption functions were estimated from two kinds of data: first, time series on consumption, savings, income, prices, and similar variables available mostly for the period after World War I; second, budget data on the consumption, savings, and income of individuals and families available from numerous sample surveys made during the past century and a half.[2] Both sources of data seemed at first to confirm Keynes's hypothesis. Current consumption expenditure was

* From *A Theory of the Consumption Function* (1957), pp. 3–6. Reprinted with the permission of the Princeton University Press.

1 J. M. Keynes, *The General Theory of Employment, Interest and Money* (New York and London: Harcourt, Brace and Co., 1936), pp. 96, 97.

2 See Faith M. Williams and Carle C. Zimmerman, *Studies of Family Living in the United States and Other Countries* (Department of Agriculture, Miscellaneous Publication 223, 1935); George J. Stigler, "The Early History of Empirical Studies of Consumer Behavior," *The Journal of Political Economy*, LXII (April 1954), pp. 95–113.

highly correlated with income, the marginal propensity to consume was less than unity, and the marginal propensity was less than the average propensity to consume, so the percentage of income saved increased with income. But then a serious conflict of evidence arose. Estimates of savings in the United States made by Kuznets for the period since 1899 revealed no rise in the percentage of income saved during the past half-century despite a substantial rise in real income. According to his estimates, the percentage of income saved was much the same over the whole of the period. The corresponding ratio of consumption expenditure to income – the constancy of which means that it can be regarded as both the average and the marginal propensity to consume – is decidedly higher than the marginal propensities that had been computed from either time series or budget data.[3] Examination of budget studies for earlier periods strengthens the appearance of conflict. The average propensity to consume is roughly the same for widely separated dates, despite substantial differences in average real income. Yet each set of budget studies separately yields a marginal propensity decidedly lower than the average propensity. Finally, the savings ratio in the period after World War II was sharply lower than the ratio that would have been consistent with findings on the relation between income and savings in the interwar period. This experience dramatically underlined the inadequacy of a consumption function relating consumption or savings solely to current income.

The conflict of evidence stimulated a number of more complex hypotheses. Brady and Friedman suggested that a consumer unit's consumption depends not on its absolute income but on its position in the distribution of income among consumer units in its community. They presented a good deal of evidence, mostly from budget data, in support of this relative income hypothesis.[4] Duesenberry based the same hypothesis on a theoretical structure that emphasizes the desire to emulate one's neighbors and the demonstration by neighbors of the qualities of hitherto unknown or unused consumption goods. In addition, he suggested that the relative income hypothesis could be used to interpret aggregate data by expressing the ratio of

[3] For a summary of Kuznets's estimates and an analysis of their implications, see Simon Kuznets, "Proportion of Capital Formation to National Product," *American Economic Review, Papers and Proceedings*, XLII (May 1952), pp. 507–526.

[4] Dorothy S. Brady and Rose D. Friedman, "Savings and the Income Distribution," *Studies in Income and Wealth*, X (New York: National Bureau of Economic Research, 1947), pp. 247–265.

consumption to income as a function of the ratio of current income to the highest level previously reached.[5] Duesenberry computed such a regression for the United States for 1929–1941 and obtained reasonably good results. Modigliani independently made essentially the same suggestion for the analysis of aggregate data, submitted it to extensive and detailed statistical tests, and concluded that it gave excellent results.[6]

Tobin has recently examined the consistency of the relative income hypothesis and the earlier absolute income hypothesis with a limited body of empirical evidence. Though he finds neither hypothesis entirely satisfactory, he concludes that the weight of evidence favors the absolute income hypothesis, and he tentatively suggests that changes in wealth may explain the rough constancy over time in the fraction of income saved.[7] Tobin's analysis is examined in more detail below (Chapter VI, section 4).

The doubts about the adequacy of the Keynesian consumption function raised by the empirical evidence were reinforced by the theoretical controversy about Keynes's proposition that there is no automatic force in a monetary economy to assure the existence of a full-employment equilibrium position. A number of writers, particularly Haberler and Pigou,[8] demonstrated that this analytical proposition is invalid if consumption expenditure is taken to be a function not only of income but also of wealth or, to put it differently, if the average propensity to consume is taken to depend in a particular way on the ratio of wealth to income. This dependence is required for the so-called "Pigou effect." This suggestion was widely accepted, not only because of its consistency with general economic theory, but

[5] James S. Duesenberry, *Income, Saving, and the Theory of Consumer Behavior* (Cambridge, Mass.: Harvard University Press, 1949). A crucial chapter of Duesenberry's book appeared earlier in *Income, Employment and Public Policy; Essays in Honor of Alvin H. Hansen* (New York: W. W. Norton & Co., 1948), pp. 54–81.

[6] Franco Modigliani, "Fluctuations in the Saving-Income Ratio: A Problem in Economic Forecasting," *Studies in Income and Wealth*, XI (New York: National Bureau of Economic Research, 1949), pp. 371–441. For further discussion of the relative income hypothesis, see Chap. VI, below.

[7] James Tobin, "Relative Income, Absolute Income, and Savings," in *Money, Trade, and Economic Growth, in honor of John Henry Williams* (New York: Macmillan Co., 1951), pp. 135–156.

[8] Gottfried Haberler, *Prosperity and Depression*, 3rd ed. (Geneva: League of Nations, 1941), pp. 242, 403, 498–502; A. C. Pigou, "The Classical Stationary State," *Economic Journal*, LIII (December 1943), pp. 343–351.

also because it seemed to offer a plausible explanation for the high ratio of consumption to income in the immediate postwar period.

One empirical study, by William Hamburger, finds that the ratio of wealth to income is closely correlated with the ratio of consumption to income, as judged by aggregate time series data for the interwar and post-World War II period.[9] Other studies, particularly some by Klein, have used budget data to investigate the role of particular kinds of wealth, especially liquid assets.[10]

This brief sketch may convey something of the flavor of the work that has been done in the past few decades on the consumption function. It cannot properly convey the wealth of detailed empirical evidence on consumption behavior that has been added during this period to earlier material, or the extraordinary number and variety of analytical studies that have been made of this evidence.

This monograph presents yet another hypothesis to explain the observed relation between consumption expenditure and income. The justification for doing so is that the new hypothesis seems potentially more fruitful and is in some measure more general than either the relative income hypothesis or the wealth-income hypothesis taken by itself. It incorporates fully the wealth-income effect and explains why the relative income hypothesis should be valid under special conditions. The hypothesis follows directly from the currently accepted pure theory of consumer behavior, seems consistent with existing empirical evidence, and has observable implications capable of being contradicted by additional evidence. Its essential idea is to combine the relation between consumption, wealth, and income suggested by purely theoretical considerations with a way of interpreting observed income data that I developed earlier for what at first glance seems a completely different purpose, namely the analysis of changes in relative income status.[11] This way of interpreting income data can be

[9] William Hamburger, "Consumption and Wealth," unpublished Ph.D. thesis at the University of Chicago; "The Relation of Consumption to Wealth and the Wage Rate," *Econometrica,* XXIII (January 1955), pp. 1–17.

[10] Lawrence R. Klein, "Estimating Patterns of Savings Behavior from Sample Survey Data," *Econometrica,* XIX, No. 4 (October 1951), pp. 438–454; George Katona, Lawrence R. Klein, John B. Lansing, and James N. Morgan, "Statistical Estimation of Economic Relations from Survey Data," *Contributions of Survey Methods to Economics* (New York: Columbia University Press, 1954), pp. 189–240.

[11] Milton Friedman and Simon Kuznets, *Income from Independent Professional Practice* (New York: National Bureau of Economic Research, 1945), Chap. V.

extended to consumption data, and in the process, the problem of changes in relative income status can be linked intimately with the problem of the determinants of consumption expenditure. The hypothesis thus enables much of the wide range of statistical evidence accumulated about the distribution of income to be brought to bear directly on the interpretation of consumption behavior.[12]

ALVIN H. HANSEN

Why is the consumption function a great contribution to economic theory?*

It has been my conviction for many years that the great contribution of Keynes' *General Theory* was the clear and specific formulation of the consumption function. This is an epoch-making contribution to the tools of economic analysis, analogous to, but even more important than, Marshall's discovery of the demand function. Just as Marshall's predecessors were fumbling around in the dark because they never grasped the concept of a demand *schedule,* so business-

[12] After completing an earlier draft of this monograph, I saw two recent papers by Franco Modigliani and Richard Brumberg on the consumption function that embody a very similar approach, but that develop its implications in a rather different direction. The similarity of approach reflects, I believe, the influence of a common intellectual environment. See Modigliani and Brumberg, "Utility Analysis and the Consumption Function: An Interpretation of Cross-Section Data," *Post-Keynesian Economics,* ed. by Kenneth K. Kurihara (New Brunswick: Rutgers University Press, 1954), pp. 383–436. Also, "Utility Analysis and Aggregate Consumption Functions: An Attempt at Integration," (to appear in a Supplement to *Econometrica*).

cycle and other theorists from Malthus to Wicksell, Spiethoff, and Aftalion, never could quite "reach port" because they did not have at hand this powerful tool. It is illuminating to re-read business-cycle and depression theories in general prior to 1936 and to see how many things settle neatly into place when one applies the consumption function analysis — things that were dark and obscure and confused without it. The consumption function is by far the most powerful instrument which has been added to the economist's kit of tools in our generation. It is perfectly true that embryonic suggestions (as also with the demand function) appear in earlier literature, but the consumption function was never fashioned into a workmanlike instrument until the *General Theory*. This, I repeat, is Keynes' greatest contribution. And in more general terms, the effect of variations in income upon all manner of economic variables has, since Keynes, become an important field for research and analysis. Income analysis at long last occupies a place equally as important as price analysis. This part of the Keynesian contribution will remain, regardless of what happens to that which relates to policy.

Time and again when I thought I had discovered this or that error in the Keynesian analysis, either on my own or at the suggestion of a critic, I have been surprised to find how often, upon examination, the point had already been anticipated and covered in the *General Theory*. I regret that I have not kept a list of these points, but only recently I came upon another interesting example which relates to the consumption function. In my *Fiscal Policy and Business Cycles* I had pointed out (p. 233 *et seq.*) that, on grounds of general reasoning and such facts as are available (Kuznets' long-run data) we may assume an upward *secular* drift in the consumption function. Later, this was elaborated more fully by Paul Samuelson. This upward secular drift is often (but erroneously) cited as proof that the consumption function analysis is not valid. Until recently, I had supposed that Keynes had overlooked the secular aspect of the problem, and it was therefore of great interest for me to discover that his particular formulation does in fact (possibly inadvertently) cover the matter in a fairly satisfactory manner. The consumption function of two periods, widely separated in time, can be made comparable by correcting for changes in prices, per capita productivity, and population increase. This would correct for the secular drift, and, if the corrected functions were found to be similar, we could say that the consumption function was stable over time. Now Keynes achieves a fairly satisfactory result by casting his consumption function in terms of wage-units. When the consumption-income schedules of two different periods are cast in terms of wage units, the effect is to correct for price and productivity changes. Thus the schedules become quite comparable over time, and we are accordingly in a position to determine whether or not a shift has in fact occurred in the consumption function.

Not only is consumption a function of income in the short run, but also in the long run. The secular upward shift in the consumption function could not occur except *as a result of* the prior rise in income. It is sometimes argued that the fact that the historical data reveal an upward secular drift in the consumption function itself proves that consumption is autonomously determined so far as the *long-run* relationship is concerned. But this is, I believe, wrong. The upward shift in the consumption function is a result of the secular rise in income. For example, the statistical evidence points to the conclusion that the *secular* upward shift in the consumption function did not occur from 1929 to 1940. In other words, the consumption schedule, measured in terms of a "full employment" income, had fallen from 1929 to 1940. Thus, at corresponding income levels (measured as ratios of a full employment income in each period), individuals saved a higher per cent in 1940 than in 1929. Had a full employment income been reached, however, in the late thirties, the higher income would have "educated" the public to higher consumption standards so that the per cent saved of the higher income might have been no higher than in 1929. The point is that it is necessary first to *achieve* the higher potential income level which progress makes possible, in order to induce people to live at a higher standard. The rising standard follows from the rising income, not the other way around.

The rôle and significance of the consumption function can be illustrated by a comparison of the *Treatise* with the *General Theory*. In the *Treatise* $\pi o = E + (I - S)$, where πo is the current income, E the normal (full employment) income, and S is the current saving which *would* be made from a normal full-employment income. Thus the current realized income is, according to the *Treatise*, less than the normal or full-employment income by the amount that current investment falls below the potential saving at full employment. But this, of course, is wrong, since it leaves out the multiplier. The missing link is supplied by the consumption function. This in a nutshell reveals one of the great advances of the *General Theory* over the *Treatise*.

In this connection it is interesting to compare Robertson's $Y_1 = Y_0 + (I_1 - S_1)$ with Keynes' $\pi o = E + (I - S)$ in the

Treatise. They bear a superficial resemblance. An important difference is that Robertson's is a period analysis which does not pretend to explain the *level* of Y_1 but only its relation to Y_0, while Keynes' (*Treatise*) equation pretends to explain the *level* of πo. By combining Robertson's formulation with the consumption function analysis (as I have done in Chapter XII in *Fiscal Policy and Business Cycles*), one can solve by the period analysis the problem attacked by Keynes in the *Treatise.* Keynes, however, chose in the *General Theory* to implement the consumption function analysis in terms of a logical or mathematical formulation involving no time-lags. Thus if the consumption function is given, the level of income is uniquely determined (time-lags assumed away) by the volume of investment.

PAUL M. SWEEZY

What has Keynes contributed to the analysis of capitalism?*

I HAVE tried to show that the opportunity to which Keynes responded was essentially a crisis in traditional economics, a crisis which was both accentuated and laid bare by the Great Depression. He was able to demonstrate that his fellow economists, by their unthinking acceptance of Say's Law, were in effect asserting the impossibility of the kind of economic catastrophe through which the world was indubitably passing. From this starting point he was able to go on to a penetrating analysis of the capitalist economy which shows that depression and unemployment are in fact the norms to which that economy tends, and which explodes once and for all the myth of a harmony between private and public interests which was the cornerstone of nineteenth-century liberalism. But Keynes stopped

* Reprinted by permission from *Science & Society* (October, 1946).

here in his critique of existing society. Our troubles, he believed, are due to a failure of intelligence and not to the breakdown of a social system; "the problem of want and poverty and the economic struggle between classes and nations," he wrote in 1931, "is nothing but a frightful muddle, a transitory and unnecessary muddle."

That Keynes held this view was, of course, no accident. He could reject Say's Law and the conclusions based on it, because he thought they were largely responsible for the muddle; but it never occurred to him to question, still less to try to escape from, the broader philosophical and social tradition in which he was reared. The major unspoken premise of that tradition is that capitalism is the only possible form of civilized society. Hence Keynes, exactly like the economists he criticized, never viewed the system as a whole; never studied the economy in its historical setting; never appreciated the interconnectedness of economic phenomena on the one hand and technological, political, and cultural phenomena on the other. Moreover, he was apparently quite ignorant of the fact that there was a serious body of economic thought, as closely related to the classical school as the doctrines on which he himself was brought up, which attempted to do these things. In Keynes' eyes, Marx inhabited a theoretical underworld along with such dubious characters as Silvio Gesell and Major Douglas; and there is no evidence that he ever thought of any of Marx's followers as anything but propagandists and agitators.

This is not the place for a review of Marxian economics. I raise the issue only in order to show that the school of thought to which Keynes belongs is rather isolated and one-sided, that some of his most important discoveries were taken for granted by socialist economists at least a generation before Keynes began to write, and that many of the most vital problems of the capitalist system are completely ignored in the *General Theory*. Marx rejected Say's Law from the outset; already before 1900 his followers were carrying on a spirited debate among themselves not only on the subject of periodic crises but also on the question whether capitalism could be expected to run into a period of permanent or chronic depression. Keynes ignores technological change and technological unemployment, problems which figure as an integral part of the Marxian theoretical structure. Keynes treats unemployment as a symptom of a technical fault in the capitalist mechanism, while Marx regards it as the indispensable means by which capitalists maintain their control over the labor market. Keynes completely ignores the problems of monopoly, its distorting effect on the distribution of income and the utilization of resources, the huge parasitic apparatus of distribution and advertising which it foists upon the economy. A socialist can only blink his eyes in astonishment when he reads that there is "no reason to suppose that the existing system seriously misemploys the factors of production which are in use. . . . When nine million men are employed out of ten million willing and able to work, there is no evidence that the labor of these nine million men is misdirected." Many other examples of the insularity and comparative narrowness of the Keynesian approach could be cited. But perhaps most striking of all is Keynes's habit of treating the state as a *deus ex machina* to be invoked whenever his human actors, behaving according to the rules of the capitalist game, get themselves into a dilemma from which there is apparently no escape. Naturally, this Olympian interventionist resolves everything in a manner satisfactory to the author and presumably to the audience. The only trouble is—as every Marxist knows—that the state is not a god but one of the actors who has a part to play just like all the other actors.

Nothing that has been said should be taken as belittling the importance of Keynes' work. Moreover, there has been no intention to imply that Marxists "know it all" and have nothing to learn from Keynes and his followers. I have no doubt that Keynes is the greatest British (or American) economist since Ricardo, and I think the work of his school sheds a flood of light on the functioning of the capitalist economy. I think there is a great deal in Marx—especially in the unfinished later volumes of *Das Kapital* and in the *Theorien über den Mehrwert*—which takes on a new meaning and fits into its proper place when read in the light of the Keynesian contributions. Moreover, at least in Britain and the United States, the Keynesians are far better trained and equipped technically (e.g., in the very important sphere of gathering and interpreting statistical data) than Marxist economists; and as matters stand now there is no doubt at all which group can learn more from the other.

But while it is right to recognize the positive contributions of Keynes, it is no less essential to recognize his shortcomings. They are for the most part the shortcomings of bourgeois thought in general: the unwillingness to view the economy as an integral part of a social whole; the inability to see the present as history, to understand that the disasters and catastrophes amidst which we live are not simply a "frightful muddle" but are the direct and inevitable product of a social system which has exhausted its creative powers, but whose beneficiaries are determined to hang on regardless of the cost. Keynes himself, of course, could never have recognized, let alone transcended, the limitations of the society and the class of which he was so thoroughly a part. But the same cannot be said of many of his followers. They did not grow up in the complacent atmosphere of Victorian England. They were born into a world of war, and depression, and fascism. Some no doubt, treading in the footsteps of the master, will seek to preserve their comforting liberal illusions as long as humanly possible. Some, in all probability, will range themselves on the side of the existing order and will sell their skill as economists to the highest bidder. But still others, while retaining what is valid and sound in Keynes, will take their place in the growing ranks of those who realize that patching up the present system is not enough, that only a profound change in the structure of social relations can set the stage for a new advance in the material and cultural conditions of the human race.

PART TWO

THE CASE FOR KEYNESIAN CONTINUITY

INTRODUCTION

As the Introduction to this volume notes, the contention that the Keynesian "revolution" is no more than a continuation of tendencies in economic theory which have deep roots in the past, bases itself on three premises. The first is the influence of Cambridge upon Keynes. Was Keynes, despite all his novelties of language and presentation, a true student of Alfred Marshall and A. C. Pigou, the Cambridge economists who towered over the scene during the first half of the 20th century? Professor Harry Johnson, of the University of Chicago, who was trained in Cambridge economics, carefully examines the continuities between Keynes' Cambridge predecessors and the Keynes of the *General Theory*, concluding that these continuities are of extreme importance.

The second premise of those who minimize the Keynesian break with the past is the anticipation of many of the important Keynesian constructions by earlier economists. Sir Dennis Robertson, as early as 1926, offered a highly "Keynesian" account of the relations between saving and investment. The marginal efficiency of capital, as Keynes himself explicitly conceded, is the child of the distinguished Yale economist, the late Irving Fisher. In the second selection in this section, a noted Swedish economist, Bertil Ohlin, argues powerfully that the Stockholm group of economists anticipated by many years the general outlines of Keynes' doctrine of income determination. Keynes has been accused by another famous Swedish economist, Gunnar Myrdal, of having practiced a certain amount of "unnecessary originality."

The third pillar of the anti-Keynesian case is the proposition that important elements of the Keynesian theory are defective. Professor A. P. Lerner of Michigan State University and Professor Gottfried Haberler of Harvard University discuss between them the view that the whole Keynesian system depends upon price and wage rigidities. This criticism may have little practical significance in western societies in which labor unions and business oligopolies do in fact prevent downward wage and price adjustments in conditions of flagging demand. But it is of considerable theoretical interest, for if Professor Haberler's position is justified, then full employment may be achieved at least as sensibly by resolute anti-monopoly and anti-union policies as by manipulation of aggregate demand. A second segment of the Keynesian system which has been severely attacked in the last generation is the liquidity preference doctrine of interest. The late Sir Dennis Robertson, once a friend and supporter of Keynes, became the severest critic especially of Keynesian theories of interest. His criticism and that of Professor Haberler constitute the concluding two portions of this section.

In sum, the position of the critics might be put this way: In most instances where Keynesian economics seem "right" and usable, Keynes simply borrowed or extended the sensible ideas of his predecessors. Where Keynes was truly novel, he also tended to be mistaken. Keynes, in other words, was accurate in his prediction that his critics would "fluctuate . . . between a belief that I am quite wrong and a belief that I am saying nothing new." Keynes' next sentence is also still relevant: "It is for others to determine if either of these or the third alternative is right."

HARRY G. JOHNSON

How important is Cambridge to Keynesian economics?*

NOT even the most ardent admirer of Keynes's powers as an expositor of economic ideas and a literary stylist would wish to have his reputation in these respects judged solely by the *General Theory*. Arresting phrases and brilliant passages there are, as everyone who has read it remembers, but the book as a whole is not easy to read and master, and it has not become easier with the passage of time. In support of this judgment one need only refer to the fact that no less than three successful books aimed at guiding the reader through the *General Theory* have appeared at intervals in the past twenty-five years – those of Joan Robinson, Dudley Dillard, and Alvin Hansen – not to speak of less well-known monographs and the countless interpretative articles which still continue to appear.

For the difficulty of the *General Theory* there are a variety of reasons. At the literary and expository level, there is the evident strain of the "long struggle of escape . . . from habitual modes of thought and expression" mentioned by Keynes in his Preface. There is also the non-rigorous Cambridge style of theorizing, the didactic Marshallian style, in which awkward complications are hidden in plain view and common sense is allowed to run away with the argument – a style which Keynes defended in his critical remarks on mathematical economics. There is the intrusiveness of Keynes the philosopher, interrupting the argument to muse on the social virtues and vices of the organized speculative markets on which he had made his own and his College's fortune, or to dilate rather pretentiously on the essential properties of interest and money. And above all there is the pervading influence of Keynes the born propagandist, with his instinct for dramatizing his ideas, and his Cassandra complex, fortified as polemicists often are by a certain obtuseness in understanding the arguments of his adversaries. . . .

* Reprinted by permission of the American Economic Association from the *American Economic Review* (May, 1961), pp. 2–17.

. . . More fundamental difficulties for the reader are inherent in the analytical content of the book. In the first place, it is difficult for a modern reader to appreciate, after twenty-five years of rapid theoretical development, the extreme limitations of the concepts then available for dealing with economic aggregates and economic dynamics. Keynes tells us that "the three perplexities which most impeded my progress in writing this book, so that I could not express myself conveniently until I had found some solution for them, are: firstly, the choice of units of quantity appropriate to the problems of the economic system as a whole; secondly, the part played by expectations in economic analysis; and thirdly, the definition of income." These perplexities reflect the absence, in the Marshallian partial-equilibrium tradition, of a clear notion of real income; the lack of a technique of dynamic analysis in the Hicksian sense, explicitly incorporating expectations; and the fact that national income accounting was in its infancy. In resolving these perplexities, Keynes was thrown strongly back on the very classical tradition he was seeking to attack. His choice of the wage unit depended on the extremely questionable classical view that labor is a uniquely homogeneous aggregate. His treatment of expectations in terms of states of expectation, and especially his distinction between short-term and long-term expectations, incorporated the pseudo-dynamics of the Marshallian distinction between short-period and long-period analysis. And his laborious discussion of the definition of income was essentially an elaboration of the Marshallian short-period theory of the firm. More fundamentally, the theory of the book is constructed on the model of Marshallian short-period equilibrium; it incorporates the same assumptions of fixity of capital stock and increasing costs and the same vagueness as to the time-period for which the analysis is relevant. This vagueness is an especially serious weakness in the *General Theory,* which attempts to bring markets with widely different speeds of adjustment – the goods market, the money market, and the labor market – into one short-period equilibrium analysis. . . .

I have dwelt on the difficulty of the *General Theory* as a book, not with the intention of leading up to the remark that in the thirties the effort required to open the oyster led those who were successful to overvalue the intellectual pearl within – which is true but trite – but to emphasize the necessity of distinguishing between the *General Theory* as one of the great books in our literature and the general theory as a system of analysis, and to enable me to place the book conveniently in its historical setting. In so doing, I have stressed the extremely Marshallian character of Keynes's theory, which I regard not as a qualification of his achievement but as a measure of the limitations which his powers of original thinking enabled him to transcend. The *General Theory* is built on Marshallian concepts. In the light of subsequent developments, it is also possible to detect Marshallian influences at a more subtle level, in Keynes's concentration on the propensity to consume. His emphasis on personal saving behavior to the neglect of corporate saving behavior reflects Marshall's inability to integrate the modern corporation into his system of economic analysis. More fundamentally, his stress on current income receipts as the prime determinant of current consumption expenditure, and particularly his deduction of the form of the income-consumption relationship from an a priori "fundamental psychological law," reflects the general weakness of the Cambridge School in dealing with capital in its relation to economic behavior. . . .

A more relevant question is whether large-scale unemployment is the typical situation of an advanced capitalist economy, as the theme and prevailing tone of the *General Theory* imply, and as the stagnationists of the late thirties insisted. It is a particularly relevant question because Keynes, unlike many of his followers, was prepared to concede that traditional quantity theory becomes relevant under full employment conditions. A conclusive argument on this question is impossible, given the changes brought about by massive peacetime armament expenditures, social security and farm support programs, aid for the underdeveloped, and the success of the Keynesian revolution in securing recognition of governmental responsibility for full employment. Nevertheless, I believe that Keynes drastically overgeneralized a particularly bad depression which was made worse by errors of economic policy. Whether this is so or not, mass unemployment of the thirties variety has not been a problem of advanced capitalist countries since the war. Stagnationists do still exist in the modern world; but they are concerned either with the underdeveloped countries or with the failure of capitalism to grow as fast as the Russians. In either case they are certainly not underconsumptionists.

If the consumption function is nowhere near as simple as Keynes made it out to be and underemployment equilibrium is a special case of dynamic disequilibrium and anyway not the chronic problem of modern capitalism, what is left of the general theory of income and employment? The contribution of the *General Theory* to modern economics is certainly not Keynes's specific model of income determination, for not only is his consumption function too simple but his theory of investment is incomplete and has had to be extended to make it usable. Rather the contribution lies in the general nature of Keynes's approach to the problem of income and employment. In the first place, he concentrated attention on the expenditure-income and income-expenditure relationships, which are much easier to understand and apply than the quantity theory relationships and which provide, in the multiplier analysis, a key to dynamic processes of change. In the second place, he provided a useful macroeconomic general equilibrium model for the analysis of a monetary economy in which capital accumulation is a specialized activity financed by the issue of marketable securities. In pure monetary theory, Keynes's crucial distinction between consumption and investment decisions has been dropped and the model refined into the four-market system comprising goods, labor, money, and "bonds" – two flows and two stocks – but the distinction remains essential to cycle and growth theory. Indirectly, also, Keynes stimulated the development of modern dynamic theory. Finally, what is most important for scientific economics but can easily be used to denigrate Keynes's work, he set out his theory in a model in which the important variables and relationships are specified in a form suitable for statistical measurement and testing. The stimulation given by the *General Theory* to the construction and testing of aggregative models may well prove to be Keynes's chief contribution to economics in the longer perspective of historical judgment, since the application of capital rather than income concepts to monetary theory may well produce better and more reliable results, and the present predominance of the income-expenditure approach prove to be a transitional stage in the analysis of economic behavior. . . .

Let me conclude by summarizing briefly the main points I have made in this lecture. The *General Theory* is an uncommonly untidy book, which bears the strong imprint of the Marshallian tradition from which it sprang. Nevertheless, it has shifted the emphasis of monetary theory to the role of money as an asset with special properties in an uncertain world and forced recognition of the fact that a monetary economy is fundamentally different from a barter economy. It provided a simple and comprehensible aggregative model of the economy, which not only facilitated the analysis of aggregative problems but greatly stimulated the development of econometric work with such models. It explained why the competitive capitalist economy does not automatically maintain a satisfactory level of employment and outlined the theory of remedial policy, thereby promoting a revolution in ideas on the responsibilities of government in such a system. On the other hand, the book was weak at a crucial point, in its neglect of the influence of capital on behavior; and its influence has been to distract attention from the role of money in the functioning of the economy. I have not, in this lecture, been able to survey the contributions of Keynes's ideas to the many specialized branches of theory — international economics, public finance, business cycles, economic growth, economic planning, to mention the major ones — where they have proved extremely fruitful. But no one could hope, in a single lecture, to take a census of the progeny of the *General Theory*.

BERTIL OHLIN

What did Knut Wicksell and his followers contribute to income theory?*

Owing to a coincidence of circumstances, already at an early stage of the depression Swedish economists came to deal with the problem of variations in employment, output and prices by means of a theoretical apparatus rather different from the price theory in economic textbooks. There are surprising similarities as well as striking differences between that apparatus and the conclusions reached in Sweden on the one hand and Mr. Keynes' "General Theory" on the other hand. Hoping that a discussion of two independent attacks on the same set of problems may throw some light on the latter, I intend in this and the succeeding paper to make some observations on these two theories. In view of the fact that the Stockholm approach and theories are only partly available in other languages than Swedish, I shall begin with some observations on this work — pointing out differences from and similarities with Keynes' position — and come in

* Reprinted by permission of the author and the Royal Economic Society from the *Economic Journal* (March, 1937), Vol. XLVII.

a second article to some critical notes on his theory. A more complete comparison between the two bodies of doctrines will have to wait until the Stockholm theory has been made available in English.

Among the circumstances which explain the present trend of theoretical analysis in Swedish economics one should, I think, first mention the writings of Wicksell, which naturally attracted more attention in Sweden than elsewhere. His *Geldzins und Güterpreise* of 1898 and his later books and papers on money contained the embryo of "a theory of output as a whole," although this fact was not clearly perceived until the late 'twenties, when Professor Lindahl presented his elaboration of Wicksell. Wicksell started from the fact that the price of an individual commodity is determined by supply and demand. If its price rises, one says that it is due to a rise in demand relative to supply. Naturally, if the prices paid for all commodities taken together rise – and thus the general price level is raised – a similar explanation should be possible. Wicksell attempted to give such an explanation through his analysis of saving and investment. Thus, he broke both with the Say doctrine that supply creates its own demand and with the accepted view that the theory of relative prices and the theory of money are two entirely different things, although he never arrived at a real unification of these theories.

Wicksell's analysis was concentrated on the process of price movements, in which credit plays a large rôle. Credit and savings have a time dimension. For this and other reasons he came to study time-using processes. The most famous is his so-called "cumulative" process, which proved to be an important "type model" of economic development, i.e., a "model sequence."

Professor Lindahl – as will be shown below – followed up the Wicksellian analysis. He showed that it was useful in a study of changes in employment and output as well as in prices. Furthermore, he showed that Wicksell's cumulative process depended on special assumptions concerning the entrepreneurs' expectations, thereby utilizing the analysis of "anticipations" which had been presented in Professor Myrdal's work, *Pricing and the Change Factor*, 1927. This work was the second of the circumstances which have vitally affected Swedish research in the field under discussion during the last decade. Myrdal discusses the influence of the uncertain future on price formation. To what extent are economic actions influenced by anticipations of future events, i.e. by expectations? In the static equilibrium price theory of the textbooks, this question had been neglected. Of the pre-depression treatises only Marshall seems to have had it in mind. If he did not make much progress himself in this field, at least he used a terminology which protects him from much of the criticism which can be directed towards other writers. In fact, Keynes' analysis of expectations in Ch. 5 — which in many ways is similar to the general view in Stockholm — can be regarded as the following up of numerous suggestions in Marshall's "Principles."

Myrdal tries to build these expectations into the static price equilibrium, and thus to give a picture of the forces existing at a certain moment of time. He does not attempt to construct a dynamic price theory which considers the *rate* of change and thus gives an account of a process in time. His theory can be regarded as the last step which a static theory can take in the direction of dynamics. In constructing his equilibrium Myrdal eliminates time from change, but not anticipations of time. In other words, he assumes a timeless adjustment, but with all friction and cost and expectations. While this may appear to be a peculiar construction, it is no doubt more realistic than the earlier static equilibrium. In any case, it enabled Myrdal to concentrate on the influence of expectations. This analysis was continued by him in Ch. V. of "Der Gleichgewichtsbegriff als Hilfmittel in der Geldtheoretischen Analyse," in *Beiträge zur Geldtheorie,* published by Prof. Hayek in 1933. He there works out in some detail the vitally important distinction between "looking forward" and "looking backward," and shows its significance more clearly than he had done before in Swedish writings and discussions. This analysis of income and capital values with the aid of *"ex-post"* and *"ex-ante"* concepts is independent of the timeless equilibrium construction which is expounded in the paper and which is similar to that used in the book of 1927. In fact, it seems most useful in a *period analysis* of the type which Lindahl and myself are using, while Myrdal views it with some scepticism.

The third decisive factor in the development of the Stockholm theory was Lindahl's book on *The Means of Monetary Policy* (published in 1930 but circulated in proof a year earlier), which I have already mentioned. He used Myrdal's expectation analysis to follow the Wicksellian line of approach by means of periods of time, perhaps somewhat under the influence of Mr. D. H. Robertson in this latter respect. Some essential parts of Lindahl's theory can be briefly indicated.

Already Wicksell had stressed that consumption purchases are governed by that part of individual incomes which people want to consume, whereas investment purchases are not directly governed by the part of income people want to save. The decisions to save and the decisions to invest are taken largely by different individuals, and there is no mechanism which guarantees that the volume of savings and of investment will always be equal. This is the very essence of the Wicksellian approach. Wicksell goes on to investigate what rôle the rate of interest can play in making them equal, and what happens when they are not made equal. Lindahl does not concentrate his attention to the same extent on the investment activity. He starts from the formula:

$$E(1 - s) = PQ;$$

E is income, s savings ratio, P the price level of consumption goods, and Q the quantity of consumption goods. Regarded as a picture of a brief period, during which equilibrium exists, this equation is implicit in the equilibrium theory of prices. It can be used, however, for an analysis of a process in time, which is divided into different periods. Lindahl studies the conditions under which the components of the equation change, the volume of consumption goods as well as their prices. In so doing he naturally has to pay a great deal of attention, although not in my opinion sufficient, to the volume of real investment. He does not confine his discussion of policy to monetary policy in a narrow sense, but analyses also the effects of changes in the financial policy of the State, e.g. the financing of deficits by borrowing. Thus, he departs a long way from the quantity theory of money approach, by which it was natural in any discussion of price problems, etc., to ask how the quantity of money could be affected. In fact, he follows Wicksell in assuming a perfect credit economy, where the quantity of money has no significance. It would carry me too far to describe his argument concerning Wicksell's cumulative process. Among other things he introduces the hypothesis of unused resources and discusses alternative "models," based on different assumptions as to the disposition to save, etc., demonstrating that they behave rather differently under the impact of the same original change. He also investigates the importance of long- and short-term interest rates, and finds Wicksell's concept of a "normal" rate of interest to be of little or no use.

These Wicksell-Myrdal-Lindahl writings were the theoretical background for the work done by four economists, who were asked by the Unemployment Committee late in 1931 to write monographs on different aspects of economic policy in relation to unemployment. What the Committee asked for amounted to an extensive treatment of the "economics of unusual resources." What will be the effect of this or that policy in conditions in which considerable quantities of the industrial agents are unemployed? The fact that the Committee put the question in this way is the fourth and last of the circumstances which influenced the direction of Swedish research in the field under discussion. I should, however, mention also the fact that Professor Bagge, a leading member of the Committee, had himself in 1930 published an excellent survey of the causes of unemployment, based on an assumption which one might call relatively constant demand in terms of money or "stable monetary conditions." Hence, it was possible for the writers of the four monographs to concentrate on the processes of general expansion and contraction of economic activity, connected with variations in total demand in terms of money. These questions were, of course, the ones which attracted the greatest general interest at this time of severe depression.

The titles of the four investigations, all published late in 1933 and early in 1934, were the following: Hammarskjöld, *On the Spread of Conjunctures;* Johansson, *Wage Development and Unemployment;* Myrdal, *The Economic Effects of Public Financial Policy;* and my own book, *Monetary Policy, Public Works, Subsidies, and Tariff Policy as Remedies for Unemployment.* In spite of considerable differences in the methods and the terminology used, there is a certain unity between the theories developed and the conclusions reached in all the reports, including also the Final Report of the Committee on *Remedies for Unemployment,* published in 1935 and written by Dr. Hammarskjöld on the basis of discussion in the Committee. This report covers on the whole the same field of theoretical problems as those in Keynes' "General Theory." While there is only a scanty discussion of the determination of the rates of interest, there is an extensive analysis of "frictional" unemployment and possible remedies, matters which are almost entirely ignored by Keynes.

The high degree of unanimity between the writers mentioned, and the fact that they were all influenced by the Wicksell-Myrdal-Lindahl writings and by Casell with regard to the anticlassical approach to price and distribution theory, make it justifiable to talk about a Stockholm school of thought. (The only non-resident in Stockholm is Lindahl, who worked in Stockholm for many years.) It must not be supposed, however, that the different members of this school agree on everything. As in my attempt below to illuminate certain aspects of the Stockholm theory I shall follow the version used by myself, I have to add that my terminology has been viewed with great scepticism by some of the younger Stockholm economists, chiefly because of my way of defining income so as to make savings and investments always equal *ex definitione.* Personally, however, I am to-day more than ever convinced that this set of definitions permits a simpler, more realistic and more easily understandable description of economic processes than the rather different definitions used by other members of the Stockholm school.

Let me begin by enumerating the characteristics of what I propose to call the "Stockholm Theory of Processes of Contraction and Expansion," meaning thereby the analysis of changes in employment, output and prices. Firstly, in the discussion of special partial processes attention is concentrated on the reaction of the economic system as a whole, i.e. possible influence on the *total* volume of output and monetary demand. Monetary theory is therefore made a part of the general price theory. The analysis has not as yet been pushed far enough to make it include a theory of business cycles. A book by Dr. Lundberg on cycle problems (*Studies in the Theory of Economic Expansion*) will, however, appear before this paper is published. Secondly, care is taken to state clearly when concepts like income and savings refer to plans or expectations for the future and when they are concerned with a period that is already finished. Thirdly, with the exception of Myrdal (whose position is not quite clear) all use a period method of analysis. In this respect the procedure is similar to D. H. Robertson's. Fourthly, as in Hawtrey's and Keynes' theories, attention is concentrated on the action of the individual entrepreneurs or consumers, and not much is said about what this involves with regard to the movements of the currency units. The exception is Dr. Hammarskjöld, who in his book of 1933 uses a velocity of money approach. Fifthly, it has been found that the reasoning to be precise enough must be casuistic. Wide use is, therefore, made of "type models" like Wicksell's cumulative process. For the construction of such models, simplifying assumptions are necessary. Hence each of them throws light on only one aspect of the processes of expansion or contraction.

BERTIL OHLIN

In the light of Swedish theory, what is a fair judgment of Keynes?*

1. *The Characteristics of the New Approach*

As I see it, the two outstanding characteristics of Keynes' theoretical system are the following. First, his reasoning runs in monetary terms instead of in "real" terms, as do the theories of Marshall, Pigou and their followers, who regard money as a "veil" which one has to take away to see things clearly. A reasoning in monetary terms does not prevent any amount of considerations of the "real" implications, whenever such considerations may be desirable, e.g. in a discussion of policy. But it has the advantage of permitting a much simpler and less sophisticated explanation of the market phenomena, which are *price* phenomena. For this reason, it has long ago been accepted by almost all schools of economic thought outside England. One sometimes gets the impression that Keynes is unaware of this. Professor P. Douglas – in well-known works – and Professor Bagge have both given us extensive treatments of wage and unemployment problems by means of reasoning in monetary terms.

The second and more important aspect of Keynes' work is that it is free from some basic assumptions tacitly made, I believe, in all systematic treatments of the pricing of commodities and productive factors, i.e. in the so-called theory of price and distribution (but not in money and cycles theory). In price theory it is assumed that the changes which are studied – e.g. changes in the supply and demand for a particular commodity – *do not react on the price system as a whole sufficiently for these repercussions outside the field of analysis to need to be considered.* A special type of repercussion, which is thereby eliminated, is that which would occur if general processes of expansion and contraction – in terms of quantity or value of out-

* Reprinted by permission of the author and the Royal Economic Society from the *Economic Journal* (June, 1937).

put — were to be started or affected by the *partial* processes under examination. E.g. in a study of the influence of a new invention the possibility that it will cause an expansion in the total volume of investment leading to inflation is not considered. This, no doubt, is a useful and fruitful method. However, this simplification would be quite absurd in the discussion of the prices and employment of the factors of production, e.g. in the determination of the wage and interest level, total employment, etc. The analysis there touches upon considerable changes in the whole price system, and is no longer chiefly concerned with a small part of it, as in the case of a particular commodity market. Hence, to avoid the consideration of such phenomena as general contraction and expansion processes, which is deferred to sections dealing with monetary and business cycle analysis, price and distribution theory proper is made to rest on the tacit assumption of what might be called *"monetary stability."* It is not possible to say what meaning is given to this in the various textbooks, for the authors do not seem to be aware of the assumption they have made. The loose idea behind their discussion has some similarity with the Say doctrine, that supply creates its own demand, but involves something more than that, for there is nothing in this assumption — that total proceeds from sales equal total costs — which prevents changes in the volume of employment and output and in price-levels. (Say's assumption rules out "profit inflation," but not "income inflation." See Keynes' *Treatise on Money*.) Perhaps the tacit assumption means "a constant sum total — in terms of money — of all industrial transactions," or "a constant national income in terms of money" or "a national income which only changes in proportion to the variation in the quantities of productive factors." Through some such assumption all other causes of incomplete employment than those connected with monopoly — including monopolistic trade union policy — and "friction" are ruled out, as well as movements in the general price-levels. Thus, the basic assumption in conventional price and distribution theory is — in my opinion — *not* one of relatively full employment. The simplification includes more than that, inasmuch as it also eliminates changes in general price-levels, i.e. that kind of process which is commonly called inflationary and deflationary.

An economic analysis on this basis ("monetary stability") can throw light upon a number of phenomena both in the labour market and in other markets. But the larger the size of the phenomena and processes considered, the greater is the probability that in the real world reactions will follow which change the total volume of output and national income, both in monetary and real terms. Hence the greater is the need for studying what this change will be. When this is done, we get a theory both of "variations in employment and output as a whole" and of movements in price-levels. Not that the conclusions concerning the pricing and employment of the factors of production, based on the assumption of "monetary stability," are entirely wrong. But only under special conditions are they sufficiently correct to be interesting, except as an introduction.

What we need is an analysis which makes no such assumption of monetary stability and which concentrates attention on the effects which all kinds of *partial processes* have on the *total* volume of employment and national income, the latter in terms of money as well as in terms of quantities of goods and services. An analysis of this type involves a consideration in price and distribution theory of those problems which have hitherto been discussed in the sections on money and business cycles in textbooks on economic principles. Thereby, the whole theory of the pricing process – which must be an account of the *time-using* process – can be given a unity which it has so far lacked. And the theory of wages, employment and interest becomes rather different from the theory built up on the basis of the "monetary stability" assumption.

The works by Lindahl, Hammarskjöld, Johansson, Myrdal and myself, that were published during the depression, represent an attempt to provide pieces of such a theory.

In a world of booms and depressions such a discussion of wages, unemployment and the rates of interest, as well as the study of all kinds of economic policy, is – as already observed – apt to be more useful than an analysis based on an assumption of some sort of "monetary stability." But it would be foolish to dispense with the latter altogether, especially as an introduction. I believe that it represents one of the most fruitful simplifications that are used in economic science. Take, e.g., the analysis of certain phenomena within the individual firm or the study of so-called "frictional" unemployment, with all its considerations of different labour qualities, the various kinds of labour mobility, etc. Certainly, a number of conclusions concerning these phenomena hold good also under less stable monetary conditions, but are more easily reached when the difficulties concerning processes of general expansion and contraction are not introduced. Such knowledge concerning the labour markets as has been reached on the basis of monetary stability has to be incorporated in any *general* theory of employment worthy of its name.

It is understandable that Keynes, in writing his treatise, has concentrated on those aspects which had to do with the changes in output as a whole, and, therefore, pays very little attention to the other aspects. But it is all the more important that the relation of his reasoning to the "old" one shall be made quite clear. In comparing his theories with what he calls the "classical" theory, Keynes seems to me to mix together and confuse the differences arising from two distinct sources, mentioned above: (1) Those which depend on the fact that what he calls the "classical" theory is a Cambridge type of analysis in "real" terms and based on certain specific assumptions as to the supply of labour, whereas he thinks in monetary terms and has given up some – though not all – of these assumptions. In this respect his attitude resembles that of Cassel and several other contemporary economists. (2) Those differences which arise because both this "classical" theory and textbooks in price and distribution theory from U. S. A., Vienna, Stockholm, etc., rest on some such assumption as I have called "monetary stability," which rules out most of the large changes in the volume of output, while Keynes' own analysis – like the books by Stockholm economists mentioned above – is concentrated on a world where there are frequent and large changes in the total volume of employment and national income. From the point of view of economists who are used to discussing in monetary terms without the special "classical" assumptions about labour supply – I believe this is true of the overwhelming majority of economists in the world since the war – the former aspect of Keynes' book is simply the long-awaited conversion of a Cambridge economist to the almost generally accepted standpoint elsewhere. It is the second characteristic which gives the book a somewhat "revolutionary" flavour, from the point of view of economic theory. In my opinion, Keynes' greatest achievement in this work lies in the fact that he attempts – and in spite of his special assumptions concerning wage inflexibility etc. to a great extent succeeds – to provide a theory for changes in total employment and price-levels, which can also be called the theory of processes of general contraction and expansion.

Of course, not all the knowledge thereby reached is new. The theories of money and business cycles, even before the present depression, and still more in recent years, have given us much knowledge concerning changes in employment and rates of interest. What Keynes calls the "classical" theory does not seem to include any theory of money and cycles, otherwise it is difficult to see how he can say that this theory has "never given a single thought" to the question: "Will fluctuations in investment have any effect on the demand for output as a whole and, consequently, on the scale of output and employment?" Business cycle theory has also taught us much about the influence of wage changes, which Keynes has failed to notice. Few economists, at least outside the Vienna school, maintained that during the severe depression of 1932–33 a reduction in wages and an increased willingness to save would have been certain to increase employment. Theoretical discussion was concentrated on the effect on the entrepreneurs' expectations about the future course of prices, wages and profits, and upon the possibility that, thereby, wage reductions would give fresh impetus to a process of deflation and contraction of economic activity. Keynes makes the statement: "The idea that we can safely neglect the aggregate demand function is fundamental to the Ricardian economics, which underlie what we have been taught for more than a century" (p. 32). While some such idea underlies the price and distribution theories — as I have already argued — it is certainly not so with monetary and cycles theory, which is based on the very opposite idea. Recent discussion in this field has resulted in conclusions — e.g. on the effects on wage changes — which can be regarded as pieces of a theory of output as a whole. Economists who have followed this discussion will find Keynes' analysis of wage reductions (on pp. 262–64) and the stress on their influence on profit expectations and the volume of investment very familiar. I am sure, therefore, that most readers of the *General Theory* have been much surprised in finding (on p. 21) that the classical theorists — this expression seems to cover all others than Keynes himself and the "underworld" of economists — "are fallaciously supposing that there is a nexus which unites decisions to abstain from present consumption with decisions to provide for future consumption." Practically all monetary theorists take account of the fact that saving accompanied by "hoarding" by some people need not lead to investment by other people. Furthermore, it is the very essence of Wicksell's theory of money and "cumulative processes" that there is no such nexus between plans to save and decisions to invest. It has become the basis for most of the recent analyses of processes of expansion and contraction. Besides, D. H. Robertson, next door to King's College — and probably not much under the influence of Wicksell — has since 1926 presented several substantial pieces of "process analysis," obviously not based on the above-mentioned fallacy. The same is true of Hawtrey. Yet Keynes (p. 32) expresses the opinion that the correct idea "could only live on furtively, below the surface in the underworlds of Karl Marx, Silvio Gesell or Major Douglas."

Let us return for a moment to the two sources of differences between Keynes and the so-called "classical" theory. It is not a mere chance that he fails to distinguish between them. In fact, he maintains explicitly that there is only one such source (pp. 21–22). The classical theory is said to depend on the assumption that "the real wage is equal to the marginal disutility of existing employment," and that "supply creates its own demand in the sense that the aggregate demand price is equal to the aggregate supply price for all levels of output and employment." But these assumptions and a third one "all amount to the same thing, in the sense that they all stand and fall together, any one of them logically involving the other two." Surely, however, the Say doctrine that supply creates its own demand has nothing to do with the psychology of the labourer. Even if a universal thirty-hours week were fixed by law, and the workers had no disutility whatsoever from work — the first assumption would then be absurd — Say's doctrine would not be affected thereby. It runs in terms of total supply and total demand, *in terms of money,* at prices which cover money costs. Conversely, even if the special assumptions concerning the supply of labour are accepted, this does not preclude an analysis of processes which are incompatible with Say's assumption.

In my opinion the vitally important distinction between the "old" type of analysis, as represented by conventional price and distribution theory, and the "new" one, represented by Keynes, the Stockholm school, and — to some extent — more or less the whole theory of money and business cycles, lies in the former's fundamental assumption (not identical with the Say doctrine) which rules out the *general* processes of expansion and contraction of employment, output and prices, thereunder all other changes in the volume of employment than those connected with monopoly and friction. The central task for economic theory to-day, towards the solution of which Keynes has made such important contributions, is the construction of a body of analysis, free from such assumptions. This amounts to a co-ordination of the theories of price, money and cycles.

2. *Keynes' Equilibrium Theory versus a Process Theory of the Stockholm Type*

If Keynes' theoretical system is modern in the respect I have touched upon above, it is equally "old-fashioned" in the second respect which characterises recent economic theory — namely, the attempt to break away from an explanation of economic events by means of orthodox equilibrium constructions. No other analysis of trade fluctuations in recent years — with the possible exception of the Mises-Hayek school — follows such conservative lines in this respect. In fact, Keynes is much more an "equilibrium theorist" than such economists as Cassel and, I think, Marshall.

The central thesis in Keynes' theory is that the volume of employment depends upon the volume of investment. As most theories of business fluctuations, in their explanation of changes in employment, concentrate attention on changes in the volume of investment, Keynes' emphasis on this latter point is not new. The novelty lies in his construction of an *equilibrium,* governed by the quantity of money, the propensity to consume, the marginal efficiency of capital, and the liquidity preference. These "independent" variables determine the rate of interest, the volume of investment and, thus, the volume of employment.

The most fundamental objection to this theory is the following. The propensity to consume expresses "the functional relationship between a given level of income in terms of wage units and the expenditure on consumption out of that income." Given a certain propensity to consume, which we can call k, we obtain $E(1 - k) = I$. The income E will vary in the same proportion as the volume of investment I. However, this holds good only in reference to a period which is finished, i.e. *ex-post.* It would have been better, therefore, to talk about the "realised consumption ratio," instead of the "propensity" to consume, expressing the relation between the volume of consumption and the realised income. $(1 - k)$ is the "realised savings ratio," which can be defined as the relation between realised income and realised saving, i.e. $\frac{E}{S}$. But the latter is the same as realised investment. Hence, $(1 - k) = \frac{I}{E}$. The equation above only expresses a truism, showing that the definitions are consistent with one another, and explains nothing. The relationship in question does not throw any light on the question "what *determines* the position of employment at any time," as Keynes claims his theory to do. Neither does it indicate an equilibrium position, towards which the economic system tends and which, if reached, will remain stable, in the absence of new changes in the independent variables. As a matter of fact, this equation holds true for *every* period, even in the most *unstable* situations.

To explain the development or the actual tendencies one must use terms which refer to the expectations, plans and actions based thereupon, an *ex-ante* terminology, as indicated in the first part of my paper in the last issue of this journal. Keynes probably has had a feeling of this, as he has used such a word as "propensity." But he has defined his terms income, investment and propensity to consume as *ex-post* concepts. Perhaps he has meant them *ex-ante?* But there is no such relation between expected income, planned consumption and planned investment as he indicates. Thus, either Keynes' reasoning is *ex-post,* and then it explains nothing, or it is *ex-ante,* and then it is entirely wrong. There is no reason why the planned investment plus the planned consumption should be equal to the expected total income for society as a whole. In other words, the planned investment will differ from the planned saving, unless they should happen to be equal by mere chance. Owing to this difference, expectations will not be fulfilled. At the end of the period people will find that their incomes, investment and savings during that period have not been what they expected them to be. Consequently, the expectations, plans and actions with reference to the next period will differ from what they were in the last period. The economic situation will change in a way which can only be explained through a study of how these differences between expectations and the actual course of events during one period influence expectations and actions in the future.

Should, however, by mere chance, planned saving and investment be equal, then expectations will come true, not for each individual or firm, but as far as total income, saving and investment are concerned. This is consistent with, but does not necessarily mean a stable situation. For people may have been expecting growing employment and income, and when these expectations are fulfilled, they may expect still further growth in income and employment. This is an exemplification of the fact that the series of events during the preceding periods may well lead to a change in planned savings or planned investment for the next period, even if expectations during the last period came true. Take another example. The volume of investment during the last period may have been influenced by old contracts which have now expired. In a thousand and one ways the situation at the beginning of the new period may be different from what it was at the beginning of the preceding period. Hence, the plans concerning savings and investment may be different also. A change in the economic situation will follow.

Let us start from a position where expectations have on the whole been fulfilled for some time and conditions have been subject only to relatively small changes. If we want to know the effects of a certain reduction in the planned volume of investment—caused, e.g., by some political changes leading to pessimism in general—then one evidently has to follow the process through a study of the successive changes in expectations and plans in actual events, in the differences between them, and in the consequent reactions of the new expectations, plans, and actions, etc. In such a sequence leading to a considerable reduction in total employment and output it is *a priori* probable that many elements in the price system will be affected. The rate of interest will probably fall as a result of the smaller willingness to invest, given a certain willingness to save. (This is in accordance with the interest theory which has been briefly indicated above, and which is different from Keynes' theory.) Furthermore, the willingness to save will decline, although this may only start at a later stage than the fall in the interest level. When people come to regard their expected income as *temporarily* unusually low, the consumption will be a greater percentage of their expected income than under other conditions. (Keynes does not accept this; see p. 95.) Much here depends on the speed with which their realised incomes and income expectations fall. Investment will be affected by the rapidity of the reactions in prices, quantities and interest rates, and in the willingness of banks to give credit to firms and individuals with declining solvency. Thus, I cannot find that the economic system tends towards a stable equilibrium described by simple reference to the change in the volume of investments. It is highly improbable that the system ever gets to a state where expectations are fulfilled, in the above-mentioned sense. Nor is there a tendency to move in the direction of some such position. And if the system should happen to get into such a position, this does not mean that it tends to remain there.

Keynes' opposite view, that his so-called equilibrium will indicate a stable position towards which the system tends – a position determined by the four independent variables – is due to the facts that he (1) *assumes* that the other three elements will not vary when the fourth one changes, even though the situation may shift from boom to depression; (2) overlooks the fundamental difference between the *ex-post* and *ex-ante* concepts, using a relation between the realised consumption and income as if it meant the planned consumption ratio. It is a consequence of this latter defect that he ignores the influence of *the speed* of the various reactions. A comparison of two equilibria – consistent with different volumes of investment – supplemented with some indications concerning certain repercussions is, of course, unable to take into account this speed of reactions, the importance of which I have illustrated in the first part of this paper and shall return to in the discussion of wage changes.

The fact that the realised savings ratio, which is identical with the relation between the volume of investment and the volume of income, varies a great deal when general business conditions change, needs no other proof than reference to the well-known fact that the production of capital goods fluctuates much more than the production of consumers' goods. Changes in the quantity of commodity stocks are small in comparison therewith, and cannot make the volume of investment reach anything like the same proportion of total income during depressions as during booms. Hence, even if the psychological willingness to save were somewhat constant, it becomes absurd to assume a relatively constant multiplier. As a matter of fact, the willingness to save fluctuates, for reasons already mentioned, and the unintentional positive or negative savings, partly connected with losses, make the realised savings fluctuate more than the planned savings, but in the same direction.

This seems to me to be a rather damaging criticism of the theory of the multiplier, and this criticism holds also if the theory is stated in terms of the *marginal* propensity to consume. Even if the marginal willingness to save – the marginal planned savings ratio – were somewhat constant during varying conditions of good and bad trade, the marginal realised savings ratio, which is identical with the relation between the increase in investment and in total production, would not be constant; for the unintentional savings come in. As a matter of fact, however, people do not decide to save the same percentage of an expected increase in income during the beginning of a recovery as they do during a boom. The necessity to pay off debts, or doubts whether the increase in income is going to be lasting, may make them decide to save 50 per cent. of the expected increase in income during the first year of recovery, whereas they would want to save only 10 per cent. at a later stage of the recovery. Thus, if we want to form some idea as to the size of the effects of an increase in investment, e.g. in public works, we can only be misled by figures concerning some normal multiplier from which the actual effect is supposed to differ only slightly. Keynes mentions some circumstances which make for changes in the marginal consumption ratio and multiplier, but the whole tendency of his argument (see p. 121) is that it varies only little. The chief reason why the multiplier theory can tell us but little about the effects of a certain increase in investment is not its fluctuation, but the fact that it leaves out of account the reaction of a certain change in the volume of output and in the general business situation on profit expectations and the willingness to invest (the marginal efficiency of capital). At the bottom of a depression public works for a moderate sum may start a recovery, which would not otherwise have come, at least for a year or two. Hence the total increase in production due to these public works may during a certain period be ten times the sums spent. In another situation an increase in public works may scare the business world to such an extent that private investment activity declines, and total output is therefore increased by less than the sum allocated to public works. Thus, the multiplicatory effect may easily—if the reactions of private investment are included—at one time be ten or more, and at another time considerably less than one.

A. P. LERNER

Why is Keynes' wage doctrine correct?*

BUT Keynes' main objection consists of a denial of the theory which is put forward as an excuse for the treatment. If money wages are reduced, it does not follow that there will be any increase in employment. A general reduction of wages will reduce marginal costs, and competition between producers will reduce prices of products. Equilibrium will be reached only when prices have fallen as much as wages, and it will not pay to employ more men than in the beginning. The workers, who are able to make agreements with their employers about their *money* wage, cannot adjust their *real* wage. If they could reduce their real wage, more would be employed; but they can only attempt to reduce their real wage by reducing their money wage at the existing price level. This, however, only brings about a proportionate fall in prices so that they are in fact not able to vary their *real* wage. That is why their unemployment is *involuntary* even if they refuse to accept a lower money wage. For that would not have the desired effect of reducing the real wage and increasing employment—it would merely remove a certain stability of prices.

* Reprinted by permission of the International Labour Office from the *International Labour Review* (October, 1936).

It has hardly been disputed that a cut in money wages, by reducing costs, will have some tendency to reduce prices, but it remains to be shown why prices should fall *proportionately* to the reduction in money wages so that there is *no* fall in the real wage and so *no* increase in employment in the manufacture of consumption goods. (Employment in investment industry depends on other factors considered below. For the time being this is taken as given.)

Whether this will be the case or not cannot be decided at all by looking merely at the effect of the wage cut upon *costs*. It is necessary also to consider the effect of the wage cut upon *demand;* whether directly or whether indirectly through the change in employment that might be initiated by the first impact of the wage cut. Until we bring this into the picture, we have not sufficient data to be able to decide what the result must be.

This has made it possible for one eminent economist to argue that a cut in money wages will increase employment, and for another eminent economist to argue that a cut in money wages will not increase employment. The first is able to show that his thesis is consistent with the cost conditions; for with a larger volume of employment – with more labor applied to the given productive equipment of society – the marginal productivity of labor is less, marginal costs are higher relatively to wages; prices (which, with the same degree of imperfection of competition, must in equilibrium bear the same ratio to marginal costs) are also higher relatively to wages, so that the workers by cutting their money wages have been successful in reducing their *real* wages. The second is also able to show that his conclusions are consistent with the cost conditions; for if there is no increase in employment, marginal costs will fall as much as wages, and prices have to fall in the same proportion as costs, so that there is no change in real wages. Further, each economist is able to accuse the other of assuming his conclusions, and then each can complain of the pot calling the kettle black. So that we have an infinite regress but no answer to our question.

The necessity of bringing in the demand side is seen even more clearly if we suppose for a moment that wages are the only item that enters into marginal costs and that marginal costs are constant. In this case there is no inverse relation between employment and real wages. If wages are cut, marginal costs fall in the same proportion as wages whether there is an increase in employment or not. There will be no fall in real wages, but that tells us nothing about the volume of employment. To get the answer to our question, we have to consider the effects of the wage cut on demand, direct as well as indirect.

The essence of the analysis whereby Keynes obtains the result that there will be no change in employment comes from a consideration of demand conditions. If there is initially an increase in employment—and, since employers very often think that a wage cut is a good thing, this impact effect is very likely—the demand conditions will be such as to bring about losses which tend to induce the entrepreneurs to curtail employment until the previous equilibrium level of employment is restored. Similarly, if the impact effect is to reduce employment, this will bring about profits which induce entrepreneurs to raise employment to the previous level.

The losses that accompany an increase in employment in the manufacture of consumption goods are due to the tendency of people whose income is increased to increase their expenditure by *less* than the increase in the outlay on their production, so that there emerges a net loss. This loss may be mitigated, but not entirely escaped, by the withholding of stocks with the intention of selling them at a more propitious moment; but this procedure, while diminishing losses, has the effect of building up superfluous stocks. The losses and the accumulation of stocks both tend to reduce employment, and these forces must persist and accumulate as long as employment remains above the equilibrium level. The whole of this phenomenon is reversed for the case where the initial effect of the wage cut is to diminish employment.

We must now consider how all this works if items other than wages enter into marginal costs. Where this is the case, these other items are payments for the use of productive resources which, in the short period, are fixed in supply. This is because they accept whatever they can get, their reward falling relatively to wages until all those that are of any use whatever are employed.

If, then, wages are reduced, the attempt to substitute labor for those other productive resources will increase employment and may reduce the earnings of these resources. As long as these earnings have not fallen in the same proportion as wages, costs and prices will not have fallen as much as wages but will have fallen more than the rewards of the other productive resources. Real wages will be lower while the real reward to the other productive factors will be greater. More men will be employed, and the total real income will be greater; since, with more men employed on the given resources, a greater real product is forthcoming. The aggregate real income of the other productive resources is increased, since the quantity employed is unchanged and the real rate of reward is increased. The aggregate real income of labor may be greater or less than in the beginning, according as the increase in employment is greater or less than the reduction in the real wage.

As long as this situation remains, prices have not fallen as much as wages have been reduced; and the workers have been able to reduce their real wages by reducing their money wages and thus to increase employment. Such a position cannot be expected to persist, but contains within itself forces which will still further reduce the rewards of the factors other than labor until costs and prices have fallen proportionately to wages, and real wages and employment are back again at the original level.

In the situation we have just described, total real income is greater than in the initial position, because more men applied to the same equipment produce more goods. There is an increase in the total real costs of the consumption entrepreneurs exactly equal to this increase in real income (since the incomes of the factors of production are the costs of the entrepreneurs). Out of this extra income, some will be saved, so that the total receipts of consumption entrepreneurs increase (in real terms) less than their outgoings. Entrepreneurs make losses which cause them to restrict their output and demand for productive resources. This goes on as long as more men are employed than in the initial equilibrium and as long as the real reward of the productive resources other than labor is greater than in the initial position. These two phenomena disappear at the same time, since the tendency to substitute labor for other productive resources, which led to the increase in employment in the first place, disappears just at the point where the real reward to the other productive factors has fallen in the same proportion as prices and wages. A new equilibrium is reached only when employment has gone back to its original level and the reward of the other resources has fallen to its old *real* level. This will only be when their prices have fallen in the same proportion as wages. As long as these have fallen only in a smaller proportion than wages, prices will be higher than before relatively to wages and lower than before relatively to the reward of the other productive resources, and the disequilibrium described will continue.

In a longer period, it will be possible to increase or decrease the supply of productive resources other than labor by varying the application of current factors of production to their manufacture, so that the above argument, which rests on the fixity of supply of productive resources other than labor, would not apply. But there will be no inducement to vary their supply since their price, determined in the longer period by their cost of production, will have varied in just the same proportion as wages. There is therefore no point in departing — except as a temporary mistake — from the initial level of employment.

This does not mean that a reduction of money wages may not have all sorts of indirect influences which ultimately react on the level of employment. There will be effects on the demand for money, on the rate of interest, on entrepreneurs' expectations of future prices (or rather of the relation of these future prices to present costs), on the distribution of wealth and spending — all these and other influences will have an effect on the number of people that entrepreneurs consider it profitable to employ — but these work in divergent directions and some of them only after a considerable interval, so that nothing can be said as to the effect of the sum of these influences on employment as a result of a reduction in wages until a complete set of assumptions have been provided as to the form and strength of these influences. Before we have all this information, we must either assume them to cancel out and say that there is no effect on employment, or else, if we wish to be more realistic, we must say that what happens to employment if money wages are reduced will depend upon other conditions, so that employment might go either up or down. Anything might happen. There is no simple rule such as the classical economists envisage relating the level of employment to the money wage.

GOTTFRIED HABERLER

What are the errors in Keynes' wage theory and attack upon Say's Law?*

LET us turn now to the interaction of the various parts and the working of the system as a whole. Even if it were true that all the materials and tools used by Keynes had been known and used before and that he did not improve them – is it not true that with their help he constructed an entirely new theoretical structure?

His demonstration that unemployment is possible in equilibrium, and his analysis of the factors determining the size and changes of employment and unemployment, are generally regarded as Keynes' most important theoretical discovery. The originality and importance of this conclusion remains unimpaired, it will be said, even if it can be demonstrated that it is derived entirely from well known premises, just as the work of a great artist remains great even if he uses well known tools and techniques.

According to a widely held view, which can be described as a sort of simplified, popular Keynesianism,[1] the possibility of underemployment equilibrium has been denied by the "classical" school and demonstrated by Keynes. The matter, however, is not so simple as that. This becomes quite clear if we reflect upon the intricate and crucial question concerning the rôle of wage (and price) rigidity in the Keynesian system. Keynes assumes that (money) wages are rigid downward. If this assumption, which is certainly not entirely unrealistic, is rigidly adhered to, most of his conclusions follow: Under-

[1] Unfortunately, there is much of this oversimplified version in the *General Theory* itself, especially in the three summarizing chapters in Book I. A sociology of the formation of scientific schools will attribute much importance to this fact. It helped to crystallize a compact group of followers by repelling and annoying some readers and attracting others.

employment equilibrium is then possible; an increase in the propensity to consume will then reduce unemployment and a decrease in the propensity to consume will produce unemployment (except if, as many classical writers assumed, the demand for idle funds, the liquidity preference proper, is wholly inelastic with respect to the rate of interest). But all this is entirely in accord with pre-Keynesian theory, although these conclusions certainly had not been generally realized and sufficiently emphasized before the appearance of the *General Theory*.

If flexible wages – "thoroughgoing competition between wage earners" (in Pigou's words) – are assumed, the situation is radically changed.[2] Obviously, under-employment equilibrium with flexible wages is impossible – wages and prices must then fall continuously, which can hardly occur without further consequences and cannot well be described as an equilibrium position.[3] This is the weak spot of the Keynesian system which is usually slurred over by the Keynesians.

As in many other cases, two different attempts to deal with this problem can be found in the *General Theory*. The first one, which belongs to what I called the oversimplified, popular version of Keynesianism, is stated early in the book (p. 11 *et seq.*), and has been too readily accepted by friend and foe. It simply says that when money wages fall, prices too will fall to the same extent; therefore real wages will remain unchanged, and since "an increase in employment can only occur to the accompaniment of a decline in the real rate of wages"[4] (p. 17), employment and unemployment will remain the same.

[2] The crucial importance of wage rigidity in the Keynesian system has been emphasized by many critics, most systematically perhaps by Franco Modigliani in his remarkable article "Liquidity Preference and the Theory of Interest and Money," EC, January, 1944.

[3] A logical possibility would, of course, be that all money expressions (prices, wages, money values) fall continuously, while the real magnitudes including employment remain the same. That would be the implication of the assumption that the Keynesian relations remain unchanged in real terms in the face of such a situation. But this case is surely too unrealistic to be seriously contemplated.

[4] Professor Hansen objects to my quoting this passage because it "fails to include the very important conditions which must be assumed to make the statement [as quoted from Keynes] true, namely, no change in 'organization, equipment and technique'; in other words, no change in productivity. Moreover, Keynes (March, 1939, EJ) explicitly repudiated the notion that employment must increase *by or through* a lowering of real wages and a movement

This solution is obviously unsatisfactory and should not be regarded as Keynes' last word. This becomes clear if we consider the solution consistent with the system as a whole which can be found in Chapter 19. There it is pointed out that a reduction in money wages will usually influence employment, but in an indirect fashion, through its repercussions upon the propensity to consume, efficiency of capital, or the rate of interest. The last-mentioned route, via the interest rate, is the one most thoroughly explored by Keynes and the Keynesians. As wages and prices are allowed to fall, money is released from the transactions sphere, interest rates fall, and full employment

along a declining so-called general demand curve for labor. In his view employment is increased by raising effective demand, thereby causing an upward *shift* in the demand curve for labor." (RES, Vol. 28, Nov., 1946, p. 185. See also Chap. XII.)

It is true Keynes did qualify his statement by the clause "with given organization, equipment, and technique" (p. 17). But in the present context the qualification is irrelevant. For in the short run (and the problem under discussion is essentially a short-run problem) Keynes always assumes "organization, equipment, and technique" constant. In EJ, March, 1939, Keynes took issue with Dunlop's and Tarshis' criticism; he there was very reluctant to give up his generalization. "I still hold," he said, "to the main structure of the argument, and believe that it needs to be amended rather than discarded" (p. 40). He tried to reconcile Dunlop's and Tarshis' findings with his theory *without* dropping the assumption of constant organization, equipment, and technique.

It is, of course, true that according to Keynes "employment is increased by raising effective demand," but he thought (with certain tentative qualifications as enumerated in the quoted article) that, by a rise in effective demand, prices are necessarily raised more and faster than money wages, and that therefore a rise in effective demand is always associated (in the short run) with a fall in real wage rates.

Keynes' reluctance to drop this hypothesis is understandable because a change of view would have required far-reaching modifications of his whole theoretical structure. He, after all, had emphasized that he was "not disputing this vital fact which the classical economists have (rightly) asserted as indefeasible" (*General Theory,* p. 17). He had argued emphatically that, if workers could effectively bargain about real wages rather than merely about money wages, unemployment could always be eliminated by wage bargains at lower wages. The disputed proposition is, thus, deeply embedded in Keynes' theory.

I personally always felt that Keynes' dogmatic insistence on the proposition in question was due to the excessively static nature of his theory. If Keynes had incorporated swings of optimism and pessimism in his theory, he would have had no difficulties in admitting that an expansion can raise not only money but also real wages (even in the short run, i.e., with organization, equipment, and technique unchanged). The plain fact is that Keynes' theory is not only more static but in several respects also more "classical" than, for example, Pigou's *Industrial Fluctuations,* where it had been pointed out that "the upper halves of trade cycles have, on the whole, been associated with higher rates of real wages than the lower halves." (1929 edition, p. 238.)

is eventually restored by a stimulation of investment. This amounts to giving up the idea of under-employment equilibrium under a regime of flexible prices and wages except in two limiting cases: Full employment may be prevented from being reached via this route, (a) if the liquidity trap prevents a fall in the rate of interest – that is to say, if the liquidity preference schedule is infinitely elastic, i.e., if people are willing to hoard unlimited amounts of money at a positive rate of interest – or (b) if investment is quite insensitive to a fall in the interest rate. Keynes himself regarded both these situations not as actually existing but as future possibilities. But what if we do regard them as actually existing – which as a short-run proposition, allowing for dynamic disturbances through unfavorable expectations, etc., would be by no means absurd? We would still not have established a stable under-employment equilibrium, for wages and prices would still continue to fall. The truth is that what would happen in this case cannot be told within the Keynesian framework, and Keynes himself would have been the last one to stick to it through thick and thin.[5] We must assume that some of the Keynesian schedules would shift. The most obvious hypothesis would seem to be that the consumption function will shift upward, because of the accumulation of liquid reserves.[6] For we must assume, it seems to me, that consumption is not only a function of income but also of wealth (and liquid wealth in particular) and of other factors which we need not discuss here and which are in fact indicated in the *General Theory* (cf. Chapters 8 and 9). A similar argument would seem to hold for the investment function.

Such extensions and modifications of the Keynesian system are entirely in keeping with Keynes' own injunction against dogmatically treating any such system as rigid and sacrosanct. He warns us that the determinant relations and magnitudes of his own system (i.e.,

[5] See the following paragraph, and footnotes 7 and 8 below.

[6] If wages and prices fall, the real value of the money stock will increase beyond all limits. I called attention to this fact and its probable effect on consumption in the first edition of my *Prosperity and Depression* (1937) without then using the term "propensity to consume." Pigou has since stressed it repeatedly. Kalecki in his brief note, "Professor Pigou on the Classical Stationary State – A Comment" (EJ, April, 1944, p. 131), in principle conceded the argument that a rise in the real value of the money stock will act as a stabilizer in a period of falling prices. He makes, however, the point that this argument applies only to gold and bank notes which are not issued by the banks through making loans or through purchases of private securities; for in the case of bank money issued against loans and private securities, the rise in the real value of money is canceled by the rise in the real value of the corresponding

the three propensities, the quantity of money, and the wage unit) are "complex, and that each is capable of being affected by prospective changes in the other";[7] he says that only "sometimes" (meaning, obviously, in certain context and over limited ranges) can they be regarded as "ultimate independent variables."[8]

It should be clear, however, that even with these modifications the theory is still much too rough for direct application and must be further elaborated and supplemented before it can be used, even in a tentative fashion, for the explanation of reality. In the short run, dynamic repercussions (unfavorable expectations, disturbances caused by bankruptcies and credit crises, etc.) must be taken into consideration. Pigou was probably right when he insisted that in a cyclical depression negative wages and prices frequently would be necessary to prevent unemployment altogether or to eliminate it quickly once it appeared.[9] The situation in the long run is radically different. Unfavorable expectations and credit crises do not last forever, disturbances caused by bankruptcies disappear, and the assumption of an infinitely elastic liquidity preference and entirely inelastic marginal efficiency of capital schedule is hardly tenable as a long-run proposition. But most economists will agree that it is not only politically easier but also economically more desirable in the long run as well as in the short, to bring about the saturation of the economy with liquid funds (if required) by increasing the quantity of money rather than by raising its value through a fall in prices. The reasons for and against that proposition (such as rigidity of long-term money

bank assets (loans and securities) which are liabilities of the public. (The net worth of the public is, therefore, not increased by the fall in the price level.)

However, as long as there is money which is not issued against private evidences of indebtedness, Kalecki's argument is invalid from the theoretical point of view, because *money* wages and prices (*note:* real wages need not fall) can always fall sufficiently to raise the real value of gold money to any level necessary, however small the (dollar) value of gold or gold certificates in circulation.

From a practical point of view, however (i.e., taking account of frictions, disturbances through expectations, etc., which are assumed away in the pure model), Kalecki's argument is important. But I need not go into that, because I believe (and I think this is also Pigou's view; cf. the Preface to his *Lapses from Full Employment*) that the model under consideration is much too simplified to be useful for practical application. (See next paragraph in the text.) It should be observed that the simplifications are essentially the Keynesian ones.

[7] *General Theory,* p. 184. What is said of *prospective* changes naturally holds also of the *actual* level and *actual* changes.

[8] *Ibid.,* pp. 246–47. Cf. also p. 297.

[9] See, e.g., his *Industrial Fluctuations,* 2nd ed. 1929, p. 225.

contracts, avoidance of industrial disputes, and unjust and undesirable changes in the income distribution, etc.) are the same ones that were discussed extensively in the literature on money throughout the nineteenth century and later in connection with the problem of whether in a progressive economy it is better to let prices fall or to keep them stable.[10] Therefore, the question ought not to constitute an issue between Keynesians and non-Keynesians.

One last word on this important subject. There is nothing in the Keynesian theory to exclude a more direct influence of wage reductions on employment. We stated above that according to Keynes this influence works via repercussions upon the consumption function, marginal efficiency of capital, and the liquidity preference (the rate of interest). In the preceding pages, we discussed the last route. But it is clearly possible that consumption and investment might be affected more directly by a reduction in wages. A reduction in the cost of certain consumption or investment goods may well stimulate demand for them, and for consumption and investment as a whole. Is it not possible that more roads, houses, hospitals, will be built when construction cost is reduced, or that the demand for certain private consumption goods will rise when their price falls?[11] Assume, to make it quite simple, that the elasticity of demand for some of those things, and therefore indirectly for labor, is unity.[12] Then the wage bill remains unchanged and there are no adverse effects through

[10] The older literature which dealt with these questions under various guises and in outmoded terminologies is extensively reviewed in C. M. Walsh, *The Fundamental Problems of Monetary Science* (New York, 1903). In the present case the argument for increasing the quantity of money and holding the price level constant is, of course, much stronger than in the historical case mentioned, because in the present case all prices (including factor prices) would have to fall, while in the other case it was for the most part a question of keeping factor prices stable and letting product prices fall *vs.* keeping product prices stable and letting factor prices rise. But the point is that many of the arguments used there are relevant for the present case too.

[11] It can hardly be denied that it is possible to raise construction cost of houses, etc. (to mention a much discussed case) to such an extent that the demand for houses is seriously restricted. It obviously follows from this proposition that a reduction of such cost (brought about by elimination of monopolistic and restrictive practices on the part of labor and contractors, etc.) may stimulate demand for homes (investment). It is generally assumed that cost-reducing innovations (e.g. prefabrication of houses) can stimulate investment. Why should then a reduction of labor costs not be capable of bringing about the same result?

[12] If the elasticity of demand is not unity, we get a much more complicated situation, which cannot be discussed here. But much of the argument could be adapted to fit that case.

a fall in consumption demand of the workers. Then employment will clearly rise. In Keynesian language we shall have to say that the marginal efficiency of capital schedule or the consumption function has gone up (which one depending upon whether the newly produced goods or installations are regarded as consumption or investment goods), and that it is this shift which has brought about the increase in employment.

One may, of course, be more or less optimistic or pessimistic concerning such favorable direct influences.[13] Keynes' theory certainly does not exclude them.

The gist of the foregoing discussion may be briefly restated from a different point of view or rather (for it amounts to nothing more) in terms of a different economic jargon. I take Paul Sweezy's brilliant obituary note on Keynes as my text.[14] Sweezy regards as the basis of the Keynesian system, and of Keynes' criticism of classical economics, the "flat rejection and denial of what has come to be known as Say's Law of Markets which, despite all assertions to the contrary by orthodox apologists, did run like a red thread through the entire body of classical and neo-classical theory. It is almost impossible to exaggerate either the hold which Say's Law exercised on professional economists or its importance as an obstacle to realistic analysis. The Keynesian attacks, though they appear to be directed against a variety of specific theories, all fall to the ground if the validity of Say's Law is assumed."[15]

What is the content of Say's Law? After the early statements of the Law by the old classical writers, the subject has become so confused by criticism and defense that neo-classical writers only rarely make use of, or allusion to, it. But I think that a careful perusal of Ricardo's formulation (which is quoted by Sweezy) should make it clear what the original meaning of Say's Law was. The passage reads as follows: "No man produces but with a view to consume or sell, and he never sells but with an intention to purchase some other

[13] It is true, Keynes calls such influences "roundabout repercussions" (p. 257) and criticizes older writers for assuming a "direct" effect of wage reductions on employment. But, as I pointed out in my *Prosperity and Depression* (2nd or later editions, p. 241), what to call direct or indirect is a purely terminological question. The most direct effect imaginable Keynes calls "roundabout" because, by definiton of the terms, it must imply a change in the propensity to consume or in the marginal efficiency of capital.

[14] *Science and Society*, Vol. X, 1946, pp. 396–406. See also Part One above.

[15] *Loc. cit.*, pp. 400–1.

commodity which may be useful to him, or which may contribute to future production. By producing then, he necessarily becomes either the consumer of his own goods, or the purchaser and consumer of the goods of some other person. . . . Productions are always bought by productions, or by services; money is only the medium by which the exchange is effected."[16]

The meaning of this original formulation of this law seems to me quite clear: It states that income received is always spent on consumption or investment; in other words, money is never hoarded, the money or expenditure stream, *MV* (in some sense), remains constant or, in still other terminology, money remains "neutral." (Note how clearly the last sentence in Ricardo's passage foreshadows what a hundred years later became known as "neutral money.")

If this straightforward, monetary meaning of the law is firmly kept in mind (which is not easy because of the *hocus pocus* accumulated over the years in later classical and anticlassical writings on the subject) two conclusions are obvious: First, Say's Law does not hold in reality; every depression is a proof to the contrary. Second, hardly any neo-classical economist who ever wrote on money or the business cycle thought that Say's Law did hold in reality. The major theme of their theories of money, interest, and the business cycle, is to analyze the causes and consequences of changes in the "intrinsic" or "extrinsic" value of money, of deviations of the money rate of interest from the equilibrium rate, and of other "aberrations from monetary neutrality," which are all different expressions for deviations of reality from the ideal state as postulated in Say's Law.

[16] *Principles of Political Economy* (Gonner ed.), pp. 273 and 275. The following quotation from Say clearly conveys the same meaning: ". . . a product is no sooner created than it, from that instant, affords a market for other products to the full extent of its own value. When the producer has put the finishing hand to his product, he is most anxious to sell it immediately, lest its value should vanish in his hands. Nor is he less anxious to dispose of the money he may get for it; for the value of the money is also perishable. But the only way of getting rid of money is in the purchase of some product or other. Thus the mere circumstance of the creation of one product immediately opens a vent for other products." Jean-B. Say (*Treatise on Political Economy,* Prinsep edition, Boston, 1921.) In later editions, Say obscured and attenuated the original meaning more and more through his attempts to meet criticisms by Malthus and Sismondi. He was forced to redefine the terms until the whole proposition became an empty tautology. See, for a brief account, P. N. Rosenstein-Rodan, "A Co-ordination of the Theories of Money and Price," *Economica,* 1936, pp. 268–9; and H. Neisser, "General Overproduction: A Study of Say's Law of Markets," JPE, Vol. 42, 1934, reprinted with revisions in *Readings in Business Cycle Theory* (1944), pp. 385 *et seq.*

A few neo-classical writers, rather naively, attributed such deviations entirely to the wickedness or incompetence of those in charge of monetary policy, but many, and as time went on more and more, of them realized that these deviations are deeply rooted in the structure of the capitalist system and cannot be easily prevented or cured by slight changes in monetary policy. Some recent neo-classical writers like Hicks and Rosenstein[17] went so far as to deny the compatibility of money and static equilibrium altogether.

Our conclusion, thus, is that there is no place and no need for Say's Law in modern economic theory and that it has been completely abandoned by neo-classical economists in their actual theoretical and practical work on money and the business cycle. That should be clear to anyone who is interested in living science (theoretical as well as realistic) and knows how to distinguish it from verbal squabbles and historical reminiscences in which economists so often indulge. The question must still be asked, however, why Say's Law was more often silently dropped rather than openly repudiated. Why did some older writers (especially Say and J. S. Mill), after having been forced to emasculate the law and to make it tautological, still pay lip service to it?

Liberal prejudices, the inability to rid oneself entirely of the assumption of a pre-established harmony of interests, were undoubtedly a factor, but it would be a bit too crude and naive to rely on this factor.[18] There is a perfectly good scientific explanation (as against a superficial explanation in terms of ideological prejudices) for the lingering doubt concerning Say's Law, the reluctance of some to repudiate it openly and the occasional attempts to uphold it in some rarefied (non-monetary) form.[19] The reason is the difficulty, upon which I commented above, of reconciling a competitive system

17 Even Hayek should be mentioned here. This becomes clear if we reflect that the extremely complicated nature of a monetary system which is neutral in his sense makes the existence of neutral money in practice utterly impossible.

18 Very sophisticated writers whom it would be utterly absurd to accuse as capitalist or orthodox apologetics (especially inasmuch as they are often on the other side of the fence as far as their political convictions are concerned) have been attracted by the intricacies of the problem and have refrained from rejecting Say's Law out of hand. Cf., for example, the articles by Neisser and Rosenstein-Rodan mentioned above and some of the literature there quoted.

19 Something like the following formulation is probably in the back of the minds of many writers: Any amount of money expenditures, however small, can buy any volume of goods offered for sale, provided prices are flexible and are low enough. This is obviously an arithmetic truism which cannot be denied, but is not very useful.

with the existence of unemployment. This difficulty has, as we have shown, not been solved by Keynes.

Summing up, we may say there was no need for Keynes to rid neo-classical economics of Say's Law in the original, straightforward sense, for it had been completely abandoned long ago. Keynes was unable, on the other hand, to solve the riddle of how to reconcile competition and unemployment which is at the root of some remaining qualms about the matter in the mind of some writers.

SIR DENNIS ROBERTSON

Why is the Keynesian theory of interest erroneous?*

WHAT is the bearing of the "liquidity preference" view of interest on the problem of the preservation of monetary equilibrium in a progressive world? What I have to say on this must be much condensed, and itself forms part of a larger story, the earlier chapters of which must be taken as told. I take for granted that the social function of banking is to procure the effective utilization of the community's thrift, and that the effective fulfilment of that function requires the execution of a certain policy with regard to the magnitude of the flow of total monetary demand. Should that policy be to cause that flow to increase in proportion to the increase in production? or in proportion to the increase in population? or in proportion, in some sense, to the increase in the aggregate stock of all factors of production? On these problems there is much to be said, and I doubt if they are capable of a perfectly clear-cut answer. But granted we have solved them in theory in some compromise fashion, we can go on to ask the further question, how far is the existence of the liquidity

* Reprinted by permission of Staples Press (London) from *Essays in Monetary Theory* (1938), pp. 45–49.

trap for thrift likely to hamper the banking system in its long-run task of executing the chosen policy, and so bringing the fruits of thrift to birth?

The question falls conveniently into three parts: (1) Under what conditions does the effective utilization of thrift require a progressive fall in the rate of interest? (2) If such a fall is required, how serious is the influence of the liquidity trap in inhibiting it? (3) How responsive is capital outlay likely to be to such a fall?

(1) Whether a fall in the rate of interest is required depends on whether the rate of invention, including the "invention" of new or resuscitated countries, keeps up with the growth of thrift, accentuated by the coming stagnation and decline of population in the west. On this last subject there is nowadays much anxiety, which I partly share. The excogitation of means to meet new wants requires more initiative than the reduplication of means to meet existing ones; and some of the new wants, e.g. for the services of manicurists and mediums, may not be of a very capital-using kind. During the nineteenth century the fundamental deformity of the Marshallian "short period" – the fact that it is not the same length at both ends, since most instruments take longer to wear out than to construct – was largely concealed from view by the growth of population, which increased the chances that the tail of each slump would be bitten off prematurely, as it were, by the head of the next boom. From many points of view the most satisfactory kind of population would doubtless be one which, while never getting any bigger, was always growing; but it is not very easy to see how that is to be achieved.

Nevertheless it is possible, I think, to be too gloomy. At no point has it been possible to divine just *where* the springs of "demand for waiting" would gush forth in the coming years. Marshall, giving evidence in the 'eighties, set forth, in a striking passage which might almost be mistaken for one of Mr Keynes's presidential addresses to the National Mutual Assurance Society, the most persuasive reasons why the rate of interest should drop rapidly in the future to 2 per cent: yet within a few years the tide had turned.

(2) The upshot of our earlier discussion of this point may be conveyed by saying that so far as the desire for liquidity is due to the "speculative" motive, i.e. the belief that the rate of interest will rise, it does not seem reasonable to expect it to be proof against a prolonged fall due to a successful accumulation of capital wealth; while so far as it is due to uncertainty in a broader sense, there are reasons for supposing the curve representing it to be much more inelastic in the long run than the short. To an enormous extent the contempo-

rary troubles of the world are due to the prolonged prevalence of a state of affairs that is neither peace nor war; real peace would do more than anything – more even than real war – not only to raise the curve of marginal productivity of investable funds, but to rotate and stiffen the roof of the liquidity trap into a straight line as vertical and rigid as Mr Chamberlain's umbrella.

(3) How responsive will capital outlay be to such fall in the rate of interest as the liquidity trap permits to occur? Can we expect the response to be at all buoyant in a community in which, owing to the rapid growth of wealth, the producers of consumption goods are continually finding their livelihood threatened by the growth of thrift? On this there are three things to be briefly said.

(i) It is as well to remind ourselves, if necessary by an arithmetic example,[1] that a decline in the *proportion of income consumed* does not necessarily mean a decline in *the rate of growth of consumption,* still less of course in the absolute amount of consumption. It is not mathematically inevitable that, in a progressive society, the producers of consumption goods as a body should live in perpetual fear of extinction.

Total Income	Consumed	Percentage Growth of Consumption	Percentage of Income Consumed	"Marginal Propensity to Consume"
10,000	8,000	—	80	—
11,000	8,400	5	76	40
12,100	8,820	5	73	38
13,310	9,261	5	70	36

(ii) Even if particular groups of producers find the demand for their wares sluggish, so that they have no motive to undertake what Mr Hawtrey has called the "widening" of capital, their best course may yet be to promote its "deepening" – i.e. mechanization may be the best response to a sagging market. From the point of view of labour this is of course a double-edged conclusion.

(iii) As I have said in the course of commentary on Mr. Harrod's exposition of the "principle of acceleration," some of the quantitatively most important forms of capital outlay in the modern world – the basic instruments of power, transport and business accommodation – are not very closely geared to the demand for particular types

[1] I am in debt to Professor Hansen (*Monetary Policy and Economic Stagnation,* p. 39) on this point.

of consumption goods, but depend rather on largely and broadly conceived estimates of the potential progress of whole regions. And fortunately it is precisely these forms of capital outlay which, because of their durability, *are* reasonably sensitive to the rate of interest; for while the difference between 5 per cent and 4 per cent may make little difference to a manufacturer contemplating the installation of rapidly obsolescent machinery, whose rate of depreciation is large relatively to either rate of interest, nobody really doubts that it does make some difference to a railway company contemplating electrification or an estate company contemplating the development of a seaside resort. It is certainly not impossible to conceive a community devoting a growing proportion of a growing income to such things without reducing the producers of consumption goods to bankruptcy – and that even though our chosen monetary policy should be one which permits the prices of finished goods to fall with the progress of technical efficiency. Indeed it is evident that broadly speaking this is what happened in that remote century which followed Waterloo – a period which even Mr Keynes seems sometimes ready to treat as an exception to the general law of entropy which he regards as governing human economic affairs.

One goes up and down in one's outlook on this matter, as on so many other things. In 1932, between the births of Mr Keynes's two big books, I find I was taking him to task for expressing in his *Treatise* a view, as I thought, too cyclical and not sufficiently secular of the problem of industrial malaise. I suppose I am a little hard to please, for I now find myself in reaction against the pessimism as to the future of enterprise which has been spread, especially apparently in certain circles in the United States, by his later book. To me, as I have said, it now seems that our present difficulties are very largely political; and that so far as they are not political, they are largely *institutional* rather than fundamental, and connected above all with the fact that our banking systems grew up in a world in which there seemed to be a natural harmony, which has proved to be illusory, between the desire of the public to keep money easily accessible in a bank and the desire of commerce and industry to borrow for *working* capital purposes. But that is a story for another occasion.

GOTTFRIED HABERLER

In the light of an inadequate theory of interest, why is the Keynesian system less original and less useful than has been claimed?*

LET us look now into the content of the system. We shall first examine the individual relationships ("functions" or "propensities") of which it is composed, and then the working of the system as a whole.

Little need be said about the marginal efficiency of capital or demand schedule for capital, because here Keynes follows conventional lines. Investment is a decreasing function of the rate of interest. In the post-Keynesian, Keynes-inspired literature, it has been more and more questioned whether the rate of interest is really such an important factor; in other words, the view has gained ground that the demand curve for capital may be fairly inelastic with respect to the rate of interest. But this is not the position of the *General Theory*, at least not of its theoretical skeleton, although Keynes in *obiter dicta* and policy recommendations frequently accepted openly or by implication the theory of lacking investment opportunities.

The liquidity preference theory of the rate of interest appeared very unorthodox and novel in 1936. The ensuing discussion has made it clear, however, that the only innovation is the assumed relationship between the rate of interest and hoarding, i.e., money held for speculative purposes (M_2) or idle deposits. (Assuming that the velocity of circulation of money, of M_1, remains the same, or if it too varies with the rate of interest, the proposition implies that the velocity of the total money stock ($M_1 + M_2$) also is positively correlated with the rate of interest.)[1] The older monetary theory assumed (more or less explicitly) that the demand for hoards is inelastic with respect to the rate of interest. Keynes assumed it to be elastic. The reasons given for this are two: (1) Hoarding is the cheaper (i.e., its opportunity cost is the lower), the lower the rate of interest; (2) the lower the rate of interest, the smaller the likelihood that it will go still lower and the greater the chance that it will rise again.[2]

The older theory was probably more realistic on this point. At any rate, cyclical and other shifts of the liquidity preference schedule are undoubtedly much more significant than its alleged negative slope. A change in the rate of interest of a few per cent, *other things being equal,* is hardly an important factor in determining the volume of hoards. The latter is determined primarily by other factors such as price expectations, general pessimism, temporary lack of investment opportunities, and so on.[3] It is true that some writers, e.g., Kalecki and James Tobin, have managed to compute beautiful correlations between the rate of interest, on the one hand, and the volume of idle deposits, on the other. But the reason is that both are (or until now

[1] This proposition was clearly foreshadowed in the earlier ("classical") literature. See, e.g., Lavington, *English Capital Market* (1921), p. 30. "The quantity of resources which [an individual] holds in the form of money will be such that the unit of resources which is just, and only just, worth while holding in this form yields him a return of convenience and security equal to the yield of satisfaction derived from the marginal unit spent on consumables, and equal also to the net rate of interest."

See also Pigou, "The Exchange-Value of Legal-Tender Money" in *Essays in Applied Economics* (1922), pp. 179–81. In his later, post-Keynesian writings Pigou always makes a specific assumption with respect to the policy followed by the banking system. In what he calls the "normal" case the banks act in such a way as to allow the quantity of money to rise and fall with the rate of interest. (See, e.g., *Equilibrium and Employment,* p. 61.)

This latter-day Pigovian approach, institutional in nature, seems to me more realistic than the Keynesian liquidity preference theory. The latter is clearly a direct descendant of the penetratingly classical Cambridge type of quantity equation (as Hicks pointed out in his paper, "Mr. Keynes and the Classics," EC, Vol. 5, 1937), and suffers from the same weakness as its parent concept, viz., excessive utilization of a marginalistic psychology in a field where a frankly institutionalistic analysis is much more fruitful.

[2] We may, perhaps, say in Hicksian terminology: The lower the rate of interest, the smaller the elasticity of expectation of future rates.

[3] I do not deny that hoarding and changes in the velocity of circulation have been much neglected in the literature, and that it is a mistake (of omission rather than commission) to regard these phenomena as data (or as occasional

were) the joint effect of the same cause, of the business cycle. It is quite easy, however, to imagine future ups and downs of business without any significant changes in interest rates. I venture to predict that in such cases we shall still find idle deposits rising in the downswing and falling in the upswing, which would prove that the correlation between hoards and interest rates does not indicate a causal relationship in the sense that people hoard more when a fall in the rate of interest makes it cheaper and vice versa.

Other propositions frequently associated with Keynes' interest theory – e.g., those concerning the connection between short- and long-term rates and the alleged floor, well above zero, below which the rate of interest cannot fall – were frequently discussed in the pre-Keynesian literature.[4] But Keynes certainly improved the analysis and utilized those theorems effectively by putting them into the broader context of a general equilibrium system.

The theory of liquidity stands in great need of further elaboration. It will be necessary to distinguish a larger number of different types of assets than just money and real goods, or money, securities, and real goods. The different types of assets have to be arranged according to their liquidity, with cash on one end of the scale, certain types of finished goods on the other end, and loans, bonds, equities, raw material, etc., in between. Much work had been done along that line before the appearance of the *General Theory*[5] (and more has been done since publication of the volume), and Keynes himself contributed important elements for a comprehensive theory, especially in his *Treatise on Money*. But these refinements, indispensable though they are for a useful application of the theory to reality, were

disturbances) instead of explaining them systematically. The point is that the level of the rate of interest as such is a comparatively unimportant factor.

Expectations of changes in interest rates are, however, a different matter. But the state of expectation is a complicated matter, and no simple formula, such as the one suggested in the preceding footnote, can do justice to its complexity.

Professor W. Fellner in his elaborate and searching investigation of the subject reaches the conclusion "that the elasticity of liquidity provisions with respect to interest rate is not likely to be high" (*Monetary Policy and Full Employment*, Berkeley, 1946, p. 200).

[4] E.g., in I. Fisher, *The Theory of Interest* (in the third approximation of his theory), or Karin Kock, *A Study of Interest Rates* (London, 1929). See, especially, Chapter VII, "Short and Long Rates of Interest."

[5] Cf., for example, Hicks "Gleichgewicht und Konjunktur" in *Zeitschift für Nationalökonomie,* Vol. 4, Vienna, 1933.

not incorporated, and were not easy to incorporate, into the body of the *General Theory* — a fact which should be kept well in mind by those who try to find empirical support for the liquidity preference theorem of the *General Theory*.[6]

[6] In all attempts at verification, the liquidity preference theory is applied to the choice between (a) cash (including bank notes and deposits) and (b) the next item on the scale, viz., shortest-term securities, in other words, between (a) money and (b) near-money (i.e., money's closest substitute). For that very limited choice (i.e., the decision whether to hold one's idle funds in cash or short-term securities) the short-term rate of interest may indeed be an important factor. But that choice is an unimportant detail as far as expenditures on goods and the volume of output and employment are concerned. And any empirical regularities found with respect to this detail cannot be regarded as a verification of the liquidity preference theorem in a rougher model which does not distinguish a whole scale of different assets with small gradations in liquidity, but only two or three types of assets.

PART THREE

THE OUTCOME

INTRODUCTION

The last selections in this volume leave unanswered the question of Keynes' permanent contribution and genuine originality. Williams and Wright take a somewhat limited view of the Keynesian "revolution." Reder and Lekachman see considerably more in the theory. It may be significant that the critics belong to an older generation than the supporters.

There is one obvious thing that remains to be said. Pro- and anti-Keynesians alike thought it worth their while to discuss Keynes in 1946 and 1961 at formal meetings of the American Economic Association. Critics and supporters have in many places and on an amazing variety of economic topics found Keynes inescapably useful or, on the other hand, sufficiently annoying to pause to attack.

In other words, Keynes is a part of the modern theory of economics. Of very few thinkers in the social sciences can similar statements be made. Even if the last contributor is right in concluding that we are now in a post-Keynesian age, it is a tribute to any economist to have even a transitory period labeled with his name.

JOHN WILLIAMS

How much of Keynes' originality was a matter of theory and how much of "opinion"?*

Keynes leaves no room for doubt that, in his view, his principle of effective demand revolutionized traditional economic theory. In the preface to *The General Theory* he speaks of "treading along unfamiliar paths," and of his long "struggle of escape." It is clear, too, that he regarded his contribution as monetary. The evolution of his thinking covered the greater part of the interwar period, and the stages in it were marked by the *Tract on Monetary Reform* (1923), the *Treatise on Money* (1930), and *The General Theory* (1936). It is clear all the way through that he was intensely concerned with the problems of his day, and particularly with those of England. In this sense all his books are dated. The first deals with the monetary disturbances of the early twenties, with a large emphasis on international monetary policy; it is dedicated to the "Governors and Court of the Bank of England, who now and for the future have a much more difficult and anxious task than in former days." The second is a monumental work – analytical, statistical, historical – whose central theme is a monetary theory of the business cycle (mainly on closed economy lines) and a policy of control of the cycle by the central bank. There is no evidence as yet of preoccupation with unemployment as a chronic tendency, booms are emphasized quite as much as depressions (nothing interested him more than our stock market boom), underconsumption and oversaving theories are given only passing reference.

In a famous passage of *The General Theory,* every sentence of which has a special relevance for his own theory, Keynes refers to "the completeness of the Ricardian victory" as "due to a complex of suitabilities in the doctrine to the environment into which it was

* Reprinted by permission of the American Economic Association from the *American Economic Review* (May, 1946), pp. 275–276, 280–283, 289–290.

projected." It was, I have always felt, a similar complex of suitabilities that accounted not only for the great impression made by Keynes's theory but also for its origin. It was not a coincidence, or a misinterpretation of Keynes, that the first great development of the theory by his disciples was the stagnation thesis, that the war was regarded as a superlative demonstration of what could be accomplished to sustain employment by a really adequate volume of effective demand, and that the weight of expectation of Keynesian economists was that we would relapse after the war into mass unemployment unless vigorous antideflation measures were pursued. There is no better short statement of the stagnation thesis than that given by Keynes: "The richer the community, the wider will tend to be the gap between its actual and its potential production; and therefore the more obvious and outrageous the defects of the economic system. . . . Not only is the marginal propensity to consume weaker in a wealthy community, but, owing to its accumulation of capital being already larger, the opportunities for further investment are less attractive." In an article in the *New Republic* which I have often quoted, Keynes concluded: "It appears to be politically impossible for a capitalistic democracy to organize expenditure on the scale necessary to make the great experiment which would prove my case . . . except in war conditions."

I find it increasingly suggested that we should distinguish between Keynes's "personal opinions" and his "theory." I agree there is often a real point in the distinction between what Keynes says and what his theory says. The book contains many *obiter dicta* which do not fit into the skeleton of his theory, and indeed provide in some cases valid grounds for objection to it. But it has been my belief that the stagnation thesis constitutes the essential content of the theory, and that as we move away from the circumstances that thesis envisaged, the difficulties for the determinancy of the theory are increased and its force as a formula for economic policy is decreased. I have, however, been skeptical of the stagnation thesis, and some of my reservations about Keynes's theory date back to that phase of the discussion. . . .

Keynes's law of the propensity to consume is the important novel feature of his theory. It has been also the most controversial. It was the main question raised by my paper on "Deficit Spending" at our meeting in 1940, by Kuznets' review of Hansen's *Fiscal Policy and Business Cycles* in 1942, and (along with his attack on equilibrium economics generally) by Burns's recent papers on Keynesian economics.

As a first statement, apart from the business cycle or other special circumstances, Keynes's "law" that as income rises consumption rises by less than unity is a plausible hypothesis; but it does not mean, necessarily, that consumption is the "passive" factor or that the consumption function is stable. These two assumptions — (1) that consumption is dependent on income and (2) that there is a "regular" or "stable" or "normal" relation between them, such that the consumption function can be derived as a given datum of the system and used as a basis of policy and prediction — constitute the essence of Keynesian economics. They bear a striking resemblance to the basic assumption of the quantity theory, that demand for money could be treated as a given factor, with the difference that, whereas that assumption was used to support the classical conclusion of full-employment equilibrium (apart from the business cycle), the new law of demand for money becomes the basis of the new equilibrium theory in which full employment is merely the limiting case. The whole structure rests upon the validity of the new law of the demand for money.

Historically, there seem to me to be ample grounds for doubting both the assumptions I have stated. They do not, for example, account for the effect of the rise of the automobile, a consumption good — or of new products generally — upon the growth of national income, where we have had a dynamic response of consumption and investment, each to the other. The application of an investment "multiplier" to consumption as a passive, given factor in order to account for such changes seems wholly unrealistic. Nor would, I think, any "dynamizing" of Keynes's technique by mathematical methods get us much further. Keynes's proposition that autonomous changes in investment determine changes in income, and hence in consumption (according to the "law"), is probably no better than its opposite, that spontaneous changes in consumption determine changes in income, and in investment. The *interdependence* of consumption and investment, each responding to the other — and both responding (spontaneously rather than systematically) to changing ideas, methods, resources — seems to me to be the essence of economic progress. But it does not lend itself readily to equilibrium analysis, which is probably the reason why it has been the concern of the historians and the more imaginative kind of statisticians rather than of the pure theorists. As between Keynesian and classical economics, however, the latter provides, in many respects, a more realistic point of departure for a study of progress.

The rise of consumer durable goods has been the outstanding economic phenomenon of our times. From the standpoint both of long-run growth and of business cycle behavior it raises serious questions for Keynesian analysis. Between the two wars expenditures on such goods were fully as large as those on capital goods, and their fluctuations fully as great; nor can we make any clear generalization as to which played the greater role in initiating cyclical changes. As "outlets for saving" they played as large a role, and the same kind of role, as new investment; nor is there any more reason for applying a "multiplier" to the one kind of expenditure than to the other. They make the Keynesian statements about "oversaving," or "institutional factors which retard the growth of consumption," or consumption as the "passive" factor, seem much less realistic than they might otherwise.

Historically, however, the growth of consumer durable goods accounts only in part for the rise in real consumption. Kuznets' paper on "Capital Formation, 1879–1938," at the University of Pennsylvania Bicentennial Conference constitutes an important landmark in the modification of Keynesian theory. He demonstrated that, while national income rose greatly during that period, standards of living rose correspondingly, and the great bulk of the increase in income went into consumption. Saving, as measured by real investment, remained a constant fraction of income, with an apparent moderate tendency in the twenties (on which he does not insist) for consumption to increase relative to income. In England before the war, according to Colin Clark's data, saving had been a diminishing fraction of a growing national income for at least a generation. Since Kuznets' paper, the "secular upward drift" of the consumption function, to which no reference is made in Keynes, has become a standard part of the statement of the consumption function. Its practical effect has been to bring the plane of discussion (the possible "gap between actual and potential production") back pretty much to where it had been before Keynes wrote, by disposing of the more serious version of his law and the one which I think he himself believed – that consumption, as a society grew richer, became a diminishing fraction of income – and limiting the stagnation thesis to a discussion of declining opportunities for investment.

But while the "secular upward drift" is now regularly included in consumption function formulae, its implications for the analysis have not been sufficiently examined. One thing it means, I think, is the point mentioned earlier, the dynamic interaction of consumption and investment. No application of the growth of investment and a multiplier to the consumption existing at the beginning of Kuznets' period, on the assumption of passivity (in the way that was so commonly being done in the thirties) could ever account for the income-consumption relation at the end; and if instead we take a historical regression of the previous relation and project it forward, we are merely begging the question.

Another part of the explanation, without doubt, has been the cost-reducing function of investment, with which, because it is too short run, Keynes's analysis does not deal. As I tried to show in an earlier paper, investment is significant, not primarily because of the money income and the employment provided by the capital-goods industries themselves, but because of the fact that by producing consumer goods in more efficient, and therefore cheaper, ways it releases consumer income for expenditure on other goods and services, and by increasing productivity per worker makes possible upward adjustments of income and increased voluntary leisure. This has been the heart of the productive process under the free-enterprise system. It points to the importance of price-wage-profits relationships which in the Keynesian system became submerged, and to the inadequacies in these directions of the Keynesian monetary and fiscal policies as the means of sustaining full employment in an advancing society. . . .

As I look back over my paper, my appraisal of Keynesian economics seems to be mostly critical. The most difficult thing to appraise is one's own bias. No doubt my appraisal has in it some element of unfavorable reaction, both to Keynes's own showmanship and his tendency to oversimplify and overstate his case, and to the sheer mass and exuberance of the claims made by his followers in his behalf. I admit all this has been working on me for a long time. Economic instability is equaled only by the instability of economists; what we need most, and often seem to have little of, is perspective. While I have no fondness for prediction, I do believe that the wave of enthusiasm for the "new economics" will, in the longer perspective, seem to us extravagant. And perhaps it will be only then that we shall be able to appraise objectively Keynes's contribution.

Beyond question it was very great. No one in our time has shaken up economists as much or been as influential in bringing economic analysis to bear on public policy. What he has given us, in particular, is a much stronger sense than we had before of the need for consumption analysis. It was the combination of the man and the times that did it. But I do have to insist again that it was policy, in Keynes's case, that led to theory, and that the weakness (as well as the strength of the impression made) lies in the overgeneralization. What we shall probably find ourselves doing is bringing back the things he temporarily submerged, the study of the processes of short- and long-run change, the emphasis on productivity, and on price-cost-profit relationships. If the conditions to which his theory was mainly directed should reappear, we shall probably find ourselves swept far beyond the kinds of remedies he favored, and forced into things he thought his theory and policies would avoid. But if we can maintain reasonable stability and, by the study of forces and relationships he largely ignored, continue to promote growth, his policies should play an effective role in a more rounded economic policy. I have sympathized all along with the idea of a cyclically unbalanced budget and with tax policies designed to promote stability and growth. But these, for Keynesians, at least before the war, were relatively mild objectives. Moreover, these are not exclusively Keynesian policies, but have been quite as popular with economists in Sweden, for example (where Keynesian economics has never really taken hold), as anywhere else.

What I find increasingly said, as the stagnation thesis recedes into the background, and the postwar questions about the consumption function, the price effects, and the like cast further doubts upon the theory as Keynes stated it, is that (and here the analogy with the quantity equation is striking) he has arranged the elements affecting the income equation in a useful form. This, I think, is true, with all the qualifications I have made. Undoubtedly, his formulation has greatly intensified the study of national income and its composition, though it is interesting that, as I indicated earlier, men like Kuznets and Colin Clark, who have pioneered such studies, dissented from his theory.

What it comes down to is that Keynes's analysis would appeal to me more if he had not claimed too much for it. As with his predecessors, it is the pretension to universality, and the equilibrium technique, that offend me, with the further point that in his case the defect seems to me worse. There is a legitimate and important role in economics for partial equilibrium analysis but the analogy with it of the Keynesian type of total equilibrium analysis seems to me most imperfect, because in the nature of the case the "other things equal" condition is invalid. Consumption, investment, total income interact, and they comprise all the "other things." Until, at least, the econometricians make more headway in deriving them (and their parts) from "within the system," this will be the nature of my skepticism.

DAVID McC. WRIGHT

Why Keynesianism is a weak doctrine in the modern world*

CONCERNING money, however, I diverge briefly to point out that Johnson like many others has missed one of the most important factual relations. The transactions motive of L_1 does not depend passively on today's actual income level but is also greatly influenced by expectations concerning tomorrow's income level – especially when the marginal efficiency of capital schedule has shifted. As Keynes said (page 299, the *General Theory*), "Effective demand corresponds to the income the *expectation* of which has set production moving" (italics added). We have here, as Keynes admitted to me, a much more direct relationship between the M.E.C. schedule, liquidity preferences, and the interest rate than usually recognized by Keynesians. (See my "Future of Keynesian Economics" in the June, 1945, issue of the *A.E.R.* In this connection, I should like to say that the demonstration that credit manipulation and monetary forces can affect the long-range rate of interest via the rate of saving would have been no "news" to the classical economist.) As usual, Keynes's end-of-the-war remarks to John H. Williams that he was trying to educate the English to the need for a higher rate of interest have been forgotten.

Returning now to profit prospects, it may shock Dr. Johnson to hear me say that I believe secular stagnation is quite possible – now! But not, I add, for Keynesian reasons. If, however, pressure groups of various sorts, plus international maladjustments, prevent adaptation and slow down both growth and investment, while on the other hand the attempt to save continues, a more or less indefinite institutional underemployment stalemate is quite possible. Incidentally, this is the actual, factual situation Keynes was trying to explain.

But here we find the real weakness of Keynesianism. For in the sort of high relative-cost plus gold outflow maladjustment we are

* Reprinted by permission of the American Economic Association from the *American Economic Review* (May, 1946), p. 19.

experiencing now and England experienced in the twenties, the real need is for greater productivity, lower costs, social adaptation. But Keynes instead draws attention off into monetary blind alleys, and keeps us from realizing, or trying to remedy, the industrial, even cultural, arteriosclerosis that is the real source of the problem. In thus misdirecting attention, Keynesianism, as usually understood, is now, as it was then, not just a negative inadequacy, but a possitive evil.

MELVIN REDER

Why did Keynes really make a difference?*

AFTER reading Professor Tarshis' interesting and useful exposition of Keynesian economics, it is difficult to understand why there were ever any anti-Keynesians. But by the same token, it is hard to understand why *The General Theory* was such a controversial and important book. The main reason for this difficulty is, I think, that Tarshis has given a rather overgenerous description of neoclassical theory.

Actually, prior to *The General Theory,* there was no coherent theory of the level of (national) income and employment in existence. Certainly, the writings of Marshall, Pigou, Robertson *et al.* abounded in references to the national dividend or income, but they hardly ever regarded it as an unknown to be determined by the equilibrium conditions of the system. They regarded it as a paremeter (entering into various supply and demand functions) which had the following properties: it increased with (1) technical progress, (2) population, and (3) the stock of capital; it also served as an

* Reprinted by permission of the American Economic Association from the *American Economic Review* (May, 1946), pp. 295–297.

indicator of welfare. That it was not treated as a variable to be determined explicitly by the equilibrium conditions of the system was not an oversight; implicitly it was already determined. It could be found (roughly) by multiplying the equilibrium quantities of the various outputs by their equilibrium prices and summing the resulting products. The level of national income could thus be derived from the equilibrium conditions of the system; but it was not, itself, an unknown.

To develop a theory of the level of income and employment (in static terms) it is necessary to suppose that the system might be in equilibrium with various levels of employment of resources; particularly of labor. Neoclassical economists failed to make this supposition and consequently they were prevented from developing a static theory of employment. For the neoclassical economist, if laborers were unemployed but wished to work at the going wage rate, it meant that the wage rate was above the equilibrium level and that the unemployment could be eliminated by a reduction in the (money) wage rate. Thus, given the usual assumptions of neoclassical theory, the level of employment in equilibrium had to be the "full employment" level.

Now it is, of course, true that in their writings on the business cycle Pigou, Robertson and others spoke (at least by implication) of changes in the level of national income and employment, and Pigou even argued that if a fall in wage rates leads to expectations of further declines, employment would decrease rather than increase. But these "dynamic" arguments were not integrated with the main body of static theory.

Keynes, in developing a theory of employment, had at least several choices. He could have accepted the neoclassical position that involuntary unemployment was incompatible with stable equilibrium, but argued that either the system did not tend to a position of stable equilibrium or that, even if it did, the position kept shifting through time and that it was the process toward the position (and not the position itself) that was interesting. To have proceeded in this fashion would not have involved contradicting the conclusions (or modifying the assumptions) of neoclassical theory; but it would have involved (1) denying that the conclusions of static theory in this area were important and (2) asserting that a dynamic theory was required. However, as Professor Tarshis' remarks would suggest, Keynes was too much of a Cambridge economist to accept this alternative.

Instead, he chose to pour his wine into Marshallian bottles. He confined himself to static theory, but determined to modify its assumptions in such a way that underemployment equilibria were possible.

To accomplish this result, he made a tour de force that has generally been considered quite unsatisfactory. He assumed that the elasticity of supply of labor was infinite (over a sizable range) with respect to the current money wage rate; i.e., that a sizable part of the work force would refuse to work for a money wage less than that currently prevailing. Consequently, if the demand schedule for labor (with respect to the money wage rate) should happen to intersect the supply curve somewhere to the left of the upper limit of the flat range (of the supply curve) part of the labor force would become involuntarily unemployed, but with no tendency for the money wage rate to fall. This is theoretically possible, but not very likely, and it is certainly not the basis for a "general theory of employment."

In the models that have been constructed by Hicks, Lange, Lerner, and others, this aspect of the Keynesian system is virtually neglected and the wage rate is taken as a datum. In Professor Tarshis' exposition this is also done in effect. By implication this defines another Keynesian model — the one with which we are most familiar and with which Keynes himself worked through most of *The General Theory*. Professor Tarshis gives an excellent brief description of this model; it is necessary to note only that it implicitly assumes the money wage rate to be constant. (Keynes's own use of wage units reflects this same assumption.) The short-run equilibrium with which Keynesian analysis is concerned is thus a short run during which the money wage rate is constant; it is also a "Marshallian" short run during which the stock of capital is constant. Whether these two different definitions of the "short run" would always be compatible, is an interesting question, but one which cannot be discussed here.

Keynes's loyalty to the neoclassical tradition is exhibited in other ways. For him, as for his predecessors, the rate of interest was the instrument by which investible funds were rationed. The rate of investment was determined by the equilibrium condition that the marginal efficiency of investment equals the rate of interest. The main difference between his theory and those that preceded it, is (in this respect) that in his system an increased desire to hold cash balances may, *ceteris paribus,* lead to an increase in the rate of interest and a resulting reduction in investment, while this could not happen in the others. Put in a somewhat more technical way, in the neoclassical system, k (in the Cambridge quantity equation) is not dependent on the rate of interest, while in the Keynesian system it is. But such differences are minor, as compared with the differences between either of these systems and those used by many econometricians in applied work. In these systems the rate of interest is virtually (sometimes completely and explicitly) abandoned as a determinant of investment. The attitude that leads to the adoption of such models has been well expressed by Hicks (*Value and Capital,* page 225): "Interest is too weak for it to have much influence on the near future; risk too strong to enable interest to have much influence on the far future." Hicks himself, for other reasons, did not wish to discard the interest rate entirely as a determinant of investment.

In these econometric models, it is implicitly assumed that the demand schedule for investible funds has, for a considerable range of yields, virtually a zero elasticity. Investment is restrained by considerations of risk, of market limitations, etc., but not by limitations of investible funds. To my way of thinking, it is quite improper to eliminate availability of funds as a determinant of the rate of investment. However, the model that seems to me correct is neither Keynesian nor neoclassical.

Such a model would be based squarely upon the fact of capital rationing. Each firm would have its own sources of capital, the supply of which would not be closely related to the rate of interest it must pay. The rate of interest would be only one, and perhaps not a very important, term in the loan contract; other terms, involving the security of the borrower, etc., might well be more important. In such a model, it would be possible to have low open-market rates coupled with a shortage of available funds for borrowers whose securities did not qualify for the open market.

This type of theory would have given Lord Keynes all the latitude he needed to develop a "general theory of employment." But to have accepted such a theory would have involved a sharp departure from the neoclassical assumption that the rate of interest allocates investible funds. That Keynes chose a path much closer to that of his predecessors is further evidence of the intellectual paternity of *The General Theory* to which Professor Tarshis has referred.

ROBERT LEKACHMAN

How useful is Keynes today?*

"He taught men to unite reason with hope . . ." HUGH DALTON

"Inflation is unjust and Deflation is inexpedient. Of the two perhaps Deflation is, if we rule out exaggerated inflations such as that of Germany, the worse; because it is worse, in an impoverished world, to provoke unemployment than to disappoint the rentier." KEYNES

IN the glance into the future that Keynes took in 1930 in his "Economic Possibilities for our Grandchildren," he had this to say about economics and economists:

> Do not let us overestimate the importance of the economic problem, or sacrifice to its supposed necessities other matters of greater and more permanent significance. It should be a matter for specialists, like dentistry. If economists could manage to get themselves thought of as humble, competent people on a level with dentists, that would be splendid!

Dentists may or may not be humble souls, and by all accounts Keynes himself aspired to virtues other than humility. All the same, the remark has its resonances in Keynes' public attitudes and intellectual strategies. The Keynes who had argued so hard during the 1920's against the Treasury view of unemployment and public works expenditures longed to convert his antagonists by persuading them that their reasoning was faulty and their techniques irrelevant. Neither malign ideology nor class selfishness was at the root of their stubbornness. "Muddle": that was the trouble. At the outset of the Great Depression, Keynes declared:

> . . . to-day we have involved ourselves in a colossal muddle, having blundered in the control of a delicate machine, the working of which we do not understand.

Keynesian politics are the politics of the excluded muddle, of better understanding, of technical responses to technical exigencies.

Such politics do not readily triumph. During the 1920's and earlier the orthodox British Treasury opinion about the efficacy of

* Reprinted by permission from *Encounter* (December, 1963), pp. 34–43.

government deficit expenditures held, in the words of the 1929 Chancellor of the Exchequer:

> that whatever might be the political or social advantages, very little additional employment and no permanent additional employment can, in fact, and as a general rule, be created by State borrowing and State expenditure.

It is a matter of record that this peculiar doctrine, which implied the existence of something like a fixed capital fund very reminiscent of the classical economists' wages fund, dominated the policies equally of Conservative Chancellors of the Exchequer like Winston Churchill and Labour Chancellors like Philip Snowden. In 1930 Snowden was capable of arguing in a House of Commons debate that "an expenditure which may be easy and tolerable in prosperous times becomes intolerable in a time of grave industrial depression. . . ." Snowden's moral was equally banal: rigid economy was absolutely essential on pain of financial collapse. This was equally Herbert Hoover's conclusion and still more the conviction (1932) of Franklin Roosevelt who virtuously attacked Hoover for his failure to balance the budget: "Let us have the courage to stop borrowing to meet continuing deficits. Stop the deficits." Thus Labour governments which drew their support from the mines and the factories were compelled by received economic doctrine to curtail even the meagre existing amounts of unemployment benefits and to abstain totally from bolder programmes of public spending.

Keynes' assault on such opinions began with an analogy: if the Treasury's view were correct, then "it must apply equally to a new works started by Morris or Courtaulds, to any new business enterprise entailing capital expenditure." Something must be wrong, thought Keynes, since no one really believed that additional private capital expenditure was unproductive:

> If it were announced that some of our leading captains of industry had decided to launch out boldly and were about to sink capital in new industrial plant to the tune, between them, of £100 million, we should all expect to see a great improvement in employment. And, of course, we should be right.

Yet, Keynes wondered, did not the capitalists just as surely divert funds from other productive enterprises as any government which undertook to expand its own expenditure? At the least the Treasury view lacked common sense. Moreover, it neglected the circumstance that there were sources of finance readily available which were perfectly capable of expanding total production, not merely altering its composition. For the savings now being paid to the unemployed as benefits to sustain them in idleness could equally be used to "equip the country." Or net foreign lending could be reduced and the funds so diverted devoted to domestic expenditure. As Keynes concluded his case,

> . . . we are left with a broad, simple, and surely incontestable proposition. Whatever real difficulties there may be in the way of absorbing our unemployed labour in productive work, an inevitable diversion of resources from other forms of employment is not one of them.

Keynes' assault was sensible enough, but it failed to convert the bureaucrats. Indeed Keynes was not even able to persuade substantial numbers of economists that his heterodox opinions were worthy of adoption. What the profession awaited before it would believe in the special efficacy of fiscal policy was the placement of this policy within the framework of a satisfactory theory of aggregate employment and aggregate economic activity.

No doubt an impatient Keynes exaggerated the degree to which his predecessors and associates had failed to grapple with such variables. For one, his friend, colleague, and ultimate critic Sir Dennis Robertson had (as early as his 1915 *Study of Industrial Fluctuation*) assumed the importance and gravity of fluctuations in employment and output. And Robertson's *Banking Policy and the Price Level* (1926) had attempted a synthesis of monetary and business cycle theory which contained many "Keynesian" elements. But Keynes' exaggeration of his own solitude pointed to the truth that economists who lacked a consistent theory of income and employment were ill-equipped to advocate consistent remedies for deficient income and inadequate employment.

Thus the years which preceded the appearance of the *General Theory of Employment, Interest and Money* in 1935 were for Keynes, a man apprenticed to practical economic problems, "a struggle of escape from habitual modes of thought and expression." These habitual modes of thought and expression were nothing less than the terminology and the assumptions of Alfred Marshall and Marshall's successor in the Cambridge Chair of Economics, A. C. Pigou. It was a struggle which occurred in the context of a Cambridge to which Keynes belonged by birth, education, intellectual affiliation, and personal sentiment. For an American it is not always easy to believe in the overwhelming significance of schools and universities in the lives of influential Englishmen, if for no other reasons than that few Americans attend boarding schools, many reside at home even during their university years, and even "Harvard" conveys meanings less portentous than "Oxbridge."

Much in Keynes' life testified to the influence of Cambridge. His father, John Neville Keynes, held the position of Registrary of Cambridge; his mother, active in Cambridge affairs, served a term as the city's mayor. Keynes himself was not only a member of the educated bourgeoisie of the Cambridge subspecies, he knew where he belonged.[1] In 1925 when he asked himself, "Ought I, then, to join the Labour Party?" he answered the question negatively. For the Labour Party struck him as a "class party, and the class is not my class."

"If," said Keynes, "I am going to pursue sectional interests at all, I shall pursue my own. . . . I can be influenced by what seems to me to be Justice and good sense; but the *Class* war will find me on the side of the educated *bourgeoisie*." His ultimate adverse judgment upon the Labour Party was based on his disbelief that "the intellectual elements in the Labour Party will ever exercise adequate control."

Cambridge must have helped to form the rationalist in Keynes and the anarchist as well. At King's, Keynes came under the influence of G. E. Moore and into the association of Lytton Strachey ("a Voltairean"), Leonard Woolf ("a rabbi"), Clive Bell ("a gay and amiable dog"),[2] R. G. Hawtrey ("a dogmatist"), and, much less frequently, E. M. Forster. Moore's *Principia Ethica* was published at the close of Keynes' first Cambridge year, 1902, and "the talk which preceded and followed it, dominated, and perhaps still dominates, everything else." What Keynes found attractive in Moore's view of the worlds is suggested in this passage from his "My Early Beliefs":

[1] Keynes belonged not only to the Cambridge of the economists but also to the Cambridge which fostered Bloomsbury. Not that Bloomsbury did not at times doubt the full credentials of this man of affairs. Bell thought that Keynes "had very little natural feeling for the arts; though he learned to write admirably lucid prose. . . ." He recalls Lytton Strachey remarking, "What's wrong with Pozzo is that he has no æsthetic sense." Pozzo was a "pet name for Maynard which Maynard particularly disliked."

As First Bursar of King's College (from 1924) Keynes pursued so active an investment policy that £30,000 of unrestricted funds which he found at the outset of his tenure had appreciated to £380,000 by the time of his death.

[2] In his cool sketch of Keynes in *Old Friends,* Clive Bell takes some issue with Keynes' recollections of the time of their meeting as well as the closeness of their University relationship. Keynes' memories are in his "My Early Beliefs" (1938). As Clive Bell recalls his friend, "Maynard laid down the law on all subjects. . . . Cocksureness was his besetting sin, if sin it can be called." But Bell also observes; ". . . his dearest friends he loved passionately and faithfully and, odd as it may sound, with a touch of humility."

> Nothing mattered except states of mind, our own and other people's of course, but chiefly our own. These states of mind were not associated with action or achievement or with consequence. They consisted in timeless, passionate states of contemplation and communion, largely unattached to "before" and "after." Their value depended, in accordance with the principle of organic unity, on the state of affairs as a whole which could not be usefully analysed into parts. For example, the value of the state of mind of being in love did not depend merely on the nature of one's own emotions, but also on the worth of their object and on the reciprocity and nature of the object's emotions; but it did not depend, if I remember rightly, or did not depend much, on what happened, or how one felt about it, a year later, though I myself was always an advocate of a principle of organic unity through time, which still seems to me only sensible. The appropriate subjects of passionate contemplation and communion were a beloved person, beauty and truth, and one's prime objects in life were love, the creation and enjoyment of esthetic experience and the pursuit of knowledge. Of these love came a long way first.

The passage, the influence, and the friends explain something of that passionate individualism in Keynes which made it natural for him during the First World War to declare himself a conscientious objector to conscription on the premise that the state had no business telling its citizens when to fight. Perhaps they explain also a curious conception of political processes which often took the shape of excessive confidence in the power of argument to transform party and national policy. The year is 1930 and Keynes is casting about for ways of combating unemployment. Up to this time his record as a free trader has been "without blemish." Here is Harrod's sequel:

> Keynes came during this year to address an undergraduate economic society in Oxford and stayed with me. . . . He told me that he intended to give us an address in favour of a revenue tariff. My face fell, and I uttered some words of deprecation. He made haste to console me. It would be all right, he assured me, because when the present phase had passed, we should return to Free Trade.

Keynes had changed his mind before and he was destined to change it again. Allied revision of reparations policy was strongly influenced by Keynesian polemics against Versailles. Parliamentary systems are more flexible than presidential systems. Still, it takes a deal of confidence in the power of reason to believe that tariffs once levied are readily to be lifted.

Yet in the major work of his life Keynes' faith in argument achieved its justification. For the composition and the dissemination of the *General Theory of Employment, Interest and Money* are twin triumphs of reason. It is a fair claim that this abstruse, stylistically uneven, occasionally wilfully confusing volume — addressed to economists only — is unique in the record of that peculiarly British subject, "political economy." No doubt educated men, even politicians, read the *Wealth of Nations* and respected its arguments. Indeed, if they were truly cultivated, they had come across the essentials of Smith's demonstration of the virtues of natural liberty in David Hume's *Political Discourses,* written two decades or more earlier. But mercantilism did not vanish in the wake of Smith's exposé of the "mercantile system," free trade had to await the repeal of the Corn Laws (1846), Speenhamland in 1795 and the Combination Acts in 1799 echoed no Smithian world view, and it remained for David Ricardo's *Principles of Political Economy and Taxation* (1817) to join an intellectually respectable technique to Smith's vision of economic freedom.

Stanley Jevons' independent discovery of the marginalist doctrine of value in 1870 (more or less coincidently with Walras in France and Menger in Germany) failed to overturn Ricardian economics and the classical pain-cost doctrine of value. In fact, as Jevons bitterly complained, he was compelled to teach his Manchester pupils Mill's version of the older economics in order to get them through their examinations. "Marginalism" became respectable in England when that archetypical insider, Alfred Marshall, released his magisterial *Principles of Economics* in 1890. The *Principles* was a reverent volume which emphasised the continuity rather than the discontinuity of economic doctrine. Even so, Marshall's quiet revolution was essentially a matter of technique rather than of economic policy — for wage reductions as cures for unemployment can be recommended with equal vigour by good Ricardian adherents to the doctrine of the wages fund *and* by good marginalist devotees of wage determination according to the economic contributions of labourers.

There was very little that practical men of affairs either in business or politics had to do differently because Marshall had superseded Ricardo and Mill.

It is the measure of Keynes' triumph that he mounted a successful assault upon an ancient set of doctrines and an equally venerable conception of respectable public policy. And the languid, intellectually sterile atmosphere of the 1930's conspired to hasten the acceptance of the Keynesian revelation. The late Joseph A. Schumpeter, no Keynesian, called "the success of the *General Theory* . . . instantaneous . . . and . . . sustained." Paul Samuelson declared that "the *General Theory* caught most economists under the age of thirty-five with the unexpected virulence of a disease first attacking and decimating an isolated tribe of South Sea islanders." "Economists beyond fifty," Samuelson went on, "turned out to be quite immune to the ailment." And the many hostile reviews – some by men under fifty – availed their writers little, for within a decade the *General Theory* had won the battle of the text-books and within fifteen years its doctrines were the staple of beginning economics instruction. In the United States *all* the leading introductory text-books of the 1950's and the 1960's have been Keynesian at least in the sense that a good half of their analytical sections is devoted to Keynesian "macroeconomics" – the definition, measurement, and determination of national income and its attendant variables, consumption, saving, and investment.[3] For most students marginalist explanations of commodity pricing and income distribution are the less interesting half of their course.

Somewhat belatedly, perhaps, the 1936 Keynes has even achieved the 1963 adherence of an American President and his (Republican) Secretary of the Treasury. It is hard to know whether to laugh or cry at the fact that Mr. Kennedy's 1963 Federal Budget marks the *first* peacetime occasion on which an American government has deliberately predicted a budget deficit, patiently explained the deficit's desirability as a conscious policy of economic expansion, and embraced fiscal policy more generally as a technique of public administration. The cries from the country's legislative cavemen have been reverberating through the Halls of Congress ever since. For there remain places in the United States where Keynes is still a radical Englishman with designs upon the Puritan Ethic.

How radical was he?

As far as technique and mode of arrangement are concerned, Keynes conserved as much as he could of what he had learned from his masters. The student of Marshall and Pigou who absorbed from them the subtleties of price determination in markets of various kinds did not discard this geometry of demonstration simply because he placed different labels on the axes (or indeed failed to draw the diagrams) and explained not how individual prices were set but how savings and investments were brought to equality. The neophyte who finally grasps the significance of "equilibrium at the level of income which corresponds to the intersection of aggregate demand and

[3] The point is one of emphasis. Keynes did not invent economic aggregates nor quite ignore individual prices. His strategy struck at the implicit assumption of his intellectual opponents that the aggregates could care for themselves if only businessmen and labourers behaved properly.

aggregate supply" has learned a lesson in the application of Marshall's technique to Keynes' problems.[4] And the mode of argument, full though it is of verbal pyrotechniques, still faithfully reflects these characteristics at the least of the Cambridge economists: simplifying assumptions are freely made. (In the most heroic of them Keynes takes "as given the existing skill and quantity of available labour, the existing quality and quantity of available equipment, the existing technique, the degree of competition, the tastes and habits of the consumer, the disutility of different intensities of labour and of the activities of supervision and organisation, as well as the social structure including the forces . . . which determine the distribution of national income.") Introspection is a faithful ally ("the fundamental psychological law, upon which we are entitled to depend with great confidence both *a priori* from our knowledge of human nature and from the detailed facts of experience, is that men are disposed, as a rule and on the average, to increase their consumption as their income increases, but not by as much as the increase in their income"). The analogies to classical mechanics upon which equilibrium analysis rests are retained ("the volume of employment is determined by the point of intersection of the aggregate supply function with the aggregate demand function"). And the institutional structure of Western capitalism is taken for granted in the main structure of the theory, if not in the *obiter dicta* and in Chapter 24.[5]

As an economic theorist Keynes' radicalism consisted largely in his choice of topics and variables. Most directly Keynes was a radical economic theorist because he placed employment at the *centre* of his macro-economics in place of price levels. And he behaved still more

[4] Even if the beginner retreats baffled by plane geometry, he can scarcely avoid absorbing a beneficial conclusion, that economic equilibrium and high unemployment are perfectly consistent phenomena, frequently to be met in the real world. This is not the least of Keynes' triumphs: the marriage of that OK word "equilibrium" with the distasteful presence of unemployment.

[5] Here indeed is the main occasion of the Marxist criticism of Keynesian economics. Thus in the course of a graceful obituary, Paul Sweezy characterised Keynes' defects as: ". . . the shortcomings of bourgeois thought in general: the unwillingness to view the economy as an integral part of a social world; the inability to see the present as history, to understand that the disasters and catastrophes amidst which we live are not simply a 'frightful muddle' but are the direct and inevitable product of a social system which has exhausted its creative power." Still more typically Paul Baran has called Keynesian economics "merely a supreme effort on the part of bourgeois economic thought to discover a way of saving the capitalist system in spite of the manifest symptoms of its disintegration and decay."

dangerously when he insisted upon the primacy of macro-economics and the subordinate position of micro-economics. These bold initiatives in turn depended upon the demolition of Say's Law,[6] the durable generalisation which denied that in competitive markets general "glut" or involuntary unemployment could occur. Keynes' polemic extended from Say's Law to A. C. Pigou's highly sophisticated adaptation of Say in his *Theory of Unemployment.*

There is more or less general agreement among economists that Keynes treated Pigou roughly and, possibly, unfairly. Nevertheless, the lasting theoretical as well as the immediate practical significance of the *General Theory* is to be found in Keynes' destruction of this "classical"[7] bogey and his demonstration that general glut and involuntary unemployment are perfectly explicable on theoretical grounds as the usual condition of economic affairs. It is paradoxical that this crucial piece of analysis is extraordinarily difficult to untangle. Keynes started by defining the premises which underlay the "classical" proposition that in competitive labour markets and competitive commodity markets a wage reduction expanded employment and a larger wage reduction expanded employment still further. Such propositions supported the still larger conclusion that aside from temporary, frictional pauses between jobs, involuntary unemployment could not exist: there was always some wage rate, however low, which corresponded to full employment.

The first "classical" wage theorem, then, amounted to no more than the statement that "the wage is equal to the marginal product of labour," or, in plainer English, the selling price of a worker's output for the period covered by his wage. So far, said Keynes, accepta-

[6] In Ricardo's formulation, Say's Law read like this: "No man produces but with a view to consume or sell, and he never sells but with an intention to purchase some other commodity. . . . By purchasing them, he necessarily becomes either the consumer of his own goods, or the purchaser and the consumer of the goods of some other person. . . . Productions are always bought by productions, or by services. . . ."

[7] As Keynes himself noted, his use of "classical" confuses:

"The classical economists was a name invented by Marx to cover Ricardo and James Mill and their *predecessors,* that is to say for the founders of the theory which culminated in the Ricardian economics. I have become accustomed, perhaps perpetrating a solecism, to include in 'the classical economists' the *followers* of Ricardo, those, that is to say, who adopted and perfected the theory of the Ricardian economics, including (for example) J. S. Mill, Marshall, Edgeworth and Prof. Pigou."

Since by 1936 "classical" was as much epithet as identification, Keynes derived obvious semantic advantages from his use of the term.

ble. What about the second "classical" theorem? "The utility of the wage when a given volume of labour is employed is equal to the marginal disutility of that amount of employment." This is a mode of re-stating a number of Benthamite propositions:

1. Work is painful
2. Additional work becomes more painful hour by hour
3. Wages please because they command pleasurable objects and services
4. But additional wages yield less pleasure, dollar by dollar, than their predecessors because they gratify tastes of diminishing intensity
5. Hence any worker will offer his services only as long as the pleasure he anticipates from his additional earnings exceeds the pain from his additional labour. In any market situation he will cease to work just before the point where additional pains match additional pleasures.

Now this marginalist extension of Bentham also implies that an individual can increase his own employment if he so revises his computation of pleasure and pain as to work more hours at existing wage rates, the same number at lower wage rates, or exchanges employment for idleness at a wage rate which he had previously esteemed unacceptable. Hence when actual unemployment characterises labour markets the fully or the partially unemployed can remedy their condition by accepting wage reductions. It follows that a situation of general unemployment must be regarded as the outcome of voluntary choices on the part of the unemployed. Although these choices may be defensible on social and historical grounds, they are not to be confused with involuntary unemployment.

It is probably just as well that ordinary citizens during the years of the Great Depression were spared full expositions of this variety. Even the vulgarisations of this doctrine which filtered down to the general public could scarcely have enhanced the public regard for economics.[8] As far as anyone could see, the experts had not advanced beyond the austere advice of *The Economist* in 1863 to the Lancashire operatives:

> No man or woman has a right to ask or has reason to expect to be paid at the same rate for their labour, when there are 250,000 operatives out of work, as when all are fully employed. No man can expect that wages should be as high per day or per piece when trade is slack and losing, as when it is brisk and profitable. A lower rate of pay is the

[8] The ultimate vulgarisation is the conclusion that the unemployed were lazy, unenterprising, or both. The late Charles E. Wilson (Secretary of Defense during the Eisenhower Administrations) aptly expressed the sentiment when he declared his preference for hunting dogs over kennel dogs.

natural and inevitable result of the present state of the Lancashire labour market. . . . No operative who had refused work at *subsistence* wages ought to be held entitled to eleemosynary aid. . . .

This was still the theory, and in economics, as in other subjects, bad theory holds the ground until better theory displaces it, even in the face of the evidence that millions of the unemployed would have gladly accepted work at almost any rate above zero. Keynes' better theory emerged in one of the denser definitions of economics. Keynes' definition of involuntary unemployment was designed to demonstrate that the phenomenon did indeed exist and that because it existed workers might be unable to increase their own employment however the wage rate varied.

"Men," said Keynes, "are involuntarily unemployed if, in the event of a small rise in the price of wage-goods relatively to the money wage, both the aggregate supply of labour willing to work for the current money-wage and the aggregate demand for it at that wage would be greater than the existing volume of employment." Or, as a translation might put the matter: People must be involuntarily unemployed if, in the event of a rise in the cost of living and a consequent drop of real wages, employers seek to hire additional workers and these additional workers willingly present themselves to be hired. For if more people will gladly labour at *lower* real wages even an economist must admit that they must have been involuntarily unemployed beforehand when real wages were *higher*. Thus Keynes granted involuntary unemployment a theoretical licence to exist.[9]

It is difficult to exaggerate the liberating effect of this reasoning. None too soon for economists, it resolved the contradiction between the evidence of their eyes that mass unemployment was not the choice of the unemployed and a theory which demanded the belief that mass unemployment was the consequence of individual reluctance to accept lower wages, trade union intransigence, business monopoly, or unsound public finance. The remainder of the Keynesian breakthrough by now is susceptible to trite summary:

[9] The point is now so trite that it is difficult to believe how startling it once appeared to argue that unemployment is the result of deficient total demand for goods not of deficient character on the part of the unemployed. Simple enough, but in an *Observer* interview (June 9, 1963), Harold Wilson recalled that the late Lord Beveridge himself failed to grasp the point: "I remember his face, very puzzled, one day after he had visited a camp for unemployed men. He said he couldn't understand why decent, able-bodied men like the ones we had seen *could* be out of work. He didn't want to face the real problem. He wanted to think in terms of frictional unemployment."

1. The total spending of the community determines total employment and individual wage bargains have very little to do with total spending,
2. If government's rôle is neutral, total spending itself consists of consumption and investment,
3. Of the two, investment is the dynamic and consumption is the passive element.

Governments can affect total spending and total employment either by:

1. Monetary policies which lower interest rates essentially by central banking operations designed to increase the supply of money, or by
2. Fiscal policies which expand the volume of total spending by increasing public outlays without raising taxes or decreasing taxes without reducing public outlays.

Lower interest rates stimulate investors who are guided by comparisons between expected profits and borrowing costs. Fiscal policies enlarge private spending if taxes are reduced and public spending if public works and public subsidies are the preferred policies.

In proper combination such policies appear capable of restoring full employment. In reverse, they are capable of dampening inflation and checking overfull employment. But above all, they restore to politicians a sense of possibility in the handling of economic difficulty and to ordinary citizens the right to hold their elected leaders responsible for continued unemployment.

One obvious measure of Keynes' success is the inability of any government to approach a general election at a time of high unemployment with the plea that public policy is helpless to control the natural forces of the economic system.

Are we now in a post-Keynesian era?

In America where Keynesianism has converted the academics (save those located in the University of Chicago and its outposts), the more sophisticated politicians, and the enlightened segment of business opinion represented by the Committee for Economic Development, the question naturally arises — as it must for Britain also — whether Keynesian doctrine of the essentially technical variety just described is adequate to the economic needs of capitalism a generation later than the *General Theory*. The programme of tax reductions and tax reforms which President Kennedy has been pressing upon a balky Congress — how he must envy a British Chancellor's power to reverse the economic engines in a single Budget Speech — actually extends the sphere of private activity and relatively diminishes that of the public sector, for it expands the spending ability of private consumers and private businessmen, not of federal instrumentalities.

If simple Keynesian fiscal policy were enough, such a programme should stimulate total spending, diminish unemployment, and restore the economy to something like full-capacity operation. Yet, few even of the Administration spokesmen believe that by itself fiscal policy will actually do the job. For the sad, uncomfortable fact may be that just about the time that the Keynesian revelation has at last won the hearts of businessmen and politicians, the nature of the economic problem has sufficiently changed to require different or, at the least, more complex remedies.

Here recent American experience is instructive. In the past five years (divided about equally between Republican and Democratic Administrations) unemployment has averaged 6 per cent. Between 1948 and 1958 the average duration of unemployment rose from 10.3 to 14.3 weeks. Between 1958 and 1962 the United States could probably have produced something like an additional $170 billion of merchandise and services in existing plants, with the assistance of available workers.

Aggregate demand may indeed have been deficient during this term of years, but, the experts agree, it has lost title as the single actor of the economic drama. Consider only six of the most popular "explanations" of American economic sluggishness.

1. *Gold drains* have compelled the American Administration to pursue policies less expansionary than domestic circumstances required.
2. *Unemployment* has been complicated by a spurt in the growth of the labour force. Expected to grow by some 1,200,000 in 1963, the labour force expanded at an average rate of only 700,000 during the 1950's.
3. *"Automation"* displaces workers more rapidly than economic expansion demands new workers. 1960's output of goods and services could have been comfortably produced in 1961 with 1.5 million fewer workers. "Automation" may or may not be a phenomenon qualitatively different from the techonological changes of the last two hundred years, but different or similar, it aggravates employment policy.
4. Partly as the consequence of automation, partly as the effect of the continuing shift from manufacturing to the service trades, *unskilled and semi-skilled jobs* are becoming relatively scarce, and managerial, technical, and professional opportunities are expanding. The skills of the labour force do not match the new job specifications. Hence older workers require retraining and younger ones need different forms of vocational education. All workers would benefit from the general education and sophistication which facilitate job changes during their career. (In the U.S. these adjustments are the more difficult be-

cause racial discrimination restricts both opportunities and education for the Negro and Puerto Rican population.)

5. *Large corporations and large unions* force prices and wages up far short of full employment. As a result, any Administration is compelled to switch from expansion to restriction well in advance of full employment. Unions force wages up more rapidly than productivity rises. Large concentrated corporations raise their prices at the breath of favourable business conditions and omit to lower them in recessions. Price stability in the United States may be purchasable only at 5–6 per cent levels of employment.
6. In the 1960's the U.S. is undergoing a recurrence of the problems of the 1930's which were postponed but not resolved by the Second World War and the consumption boom which followed it. In common with other mature societies, notably England, the U.S. is caught in a "contradiction" between the bounding forces of production and the feebler capacities to consume which a continuingly inegalitarian distribution of income renders inevitable. Under capitalism, deficiencies of aggregate demand are always either present or imminent. (A spate of recent American studies, notably those of Lampman, Miller, Harrington, and Kolko, have supported this proposition with evidence that the trend towards diminished inequality of income halted about the same time as the conclusion of the Second World War.)

What is notable about these varied explanations of the American situation is this: with the important exception of the last one, they have comparatively *little* to do with Keynesian diagnoses. The first argument is the venerable gold standard justification of internal deflation. In the 1960's its only novelty is contained in the fact that no nation is actually on the gold standard. Explanations 2, 3, and 4 are either connected with "accidental," temporary circumstances like unusual increases in the size of the labour force or with frictional impediments such as imperfections of labour market organisation. Number 5, the popular post-war emphasis upon cost-push inflation, bases itself on the behaviour of large economic units like the giant American corporation (in a good year General Motors sales are larger than the national income of Yugoslavia), or the huge trade unions. But, to say the least, such behaviour is imperfectly comprehended within the Keynesian conceptual framework and Keynes himself, by abstracting from the degree of competition, in effect denied its importance to his analysis.

It is the sixth account of American economic difficulty which is the most interesting, if not necessarily the most convincing. It echoes the still durable doctrine of secular stagnation, now in disrepute among most economists. Indeed, in the version which Alvin Hansen and his followers made familiar in the 1930's, secular stagnation is untenable as a hypothesis, for the "secular stagnationists" derived their predictions of (more or less) permanent inadequacies of aggregate demand from the "slow-down in population growth" (which summarised the demographic experience of the last part of the 19th and the first third of the 20th century). In the U.S. the 1950 and the 1960 Censuses put the quietus on this line of argument. But, shorn of its demography, secular stagnation is a convenient label for *any* persistent tendency of aggregate demand and aggregate supply to reach equilibrium at less than full employment levels of national income.

It is worth seeing how much in Keynes supports this more generalised version of secular stagnation. Plainly the Keynes who is now in vogue is an essentially *conservative* figure completely devoted to the proposition that the proper application of intelligent monetary and fiscal policies can maintain intact the current institutional arrangements of Western capitalism. Indeed, regarded solely as an analytical apparatus, Keynesian macro-economics plausibly supports such interpretations of Keynes' essential meaning.

All the same, there is *another* Keynes present both in the *General Theory* and in earlier writings. This is a less optimistic and a less capitalist Keynes. Certainly as early as 1920 and the *Economic Consequences of the Peace,* Keynes was already emphasising the fragility of capitalistic arrangements. As an example, here are his comments on the delicate balance of forces which facilitated the social harmonies of 1870–1914:

> While there was some continuous improvement in the daily conditions of life of the mass of the population, Society was so framed as to throw a great part of the increased income into the control of the class least likely to consume it. . . . This remarkable system depended for its growth on a double bluff of deception. On the one hand, the labouring classes accepted from ignorance or powerlessness, or were compelled, persuaded or cajoled by custom, convention, authority and the well-established order of Society into accepting a situation in which they and Nature and the capitalists were co-operating to produce. And on the other hand the capitalist classes were allowed to call the best part of the cake theirs and were theoretically free to consume it, on the tacit underlying condition that they consume very little of it in practice.

As Keynes described the operations of this system of "double bluff," a good deal depended upon the mystique of the gold standard and the astute, secretive central bankers who worked its controls. Much rested on a complex international division of labour which required comparatively free trade among the nations. The First World War slaughtered the gold standard, disrupted the international division of labour, and dealt a mortal blow to free trade. Probably it deranged the social harmonies into the bargain.

Keynes' anxious observation of English economic troubles during the 1920's led him in his *Treatise on Money* (1930) to diagnose England's economic ailment as "over-saving." In part, the difficulty was geriatric: "England is an old country. . . . The population will soon cease to grow. Our habits and institutions keep us, in spite of all claims to the contrary, a thrifty people." Now thrift in itself is not disastrous to full employment if its accompaniment is vigorous investment. Such indeed was the combination which explained for Keynes the economic successes of the period which preceded the First World War. But by the time Keynes came to write the *General Theory,* he had begun to question the plausibility of high investment:

> To-day and presumably for the future, the schedule of the marginal efficiency of capital is for a variety of reasons much lower than it was in the nineteenth century. The acuteness and the peculiarity of our contemporary problems arise, therefore, out of the possibility that the average rate of interest which will allow a reasonable average level of employment is one so unacceptable to wealth-owners that it cannot be readily established by manipulating the quantity of money.

What therapy is possible? The Keynesian treatment most acceptable to the conservative is variation of interest rates. But suppose, as the quotation argues, interest rates must be forced down so low to stimulate sluggish investors that the wealth-owners will not part with their wealth for so small a reward. In such circumstances the money which central banking authorities can so easily create will not flow into productive investment. If, in addition, the character of the demand for new investment funds is such that interest rate variation has little influence on the volume of new investment, then even direct lending by government agencies at rates of interest little higher than zero will have little impact on the scale of investment in the first instance and the level of national income and employment in the second.

Many of the *obiter dicta* scattered through the *General Theory* uneasily contemplate the possibility that extra money will disappear in the liquidity trap, interest rates will not fall low enough to evoke additional investment, and the marginal efficiency of capital (the expected profits from investment) will remain stubbornly low. Where such conditions obtain, monetary policy promises little or nothing.

What else is there? Keynes' clearest statement of the alternative occurs near the end of the concluding chapter of the *General Theory*. It is a remarkable combination of Keynes' characteristic emphases on diagnosis and treatment:

> In some other respects the foregoing theory is moderately conservative in its implications. For whilst it indicates the vital importance of establishing certain central controls in matters which are now left in the main to individual initiative, there are wide fields of activity which are unaffected. The State will have to exercise a guiding influence on the propensity to consume partly through its scheme of taxation, partly by fixing the rate of interest, and partly, perhaps, in other ways.
>
> Furthermore, it seems unlikely that the influence of banking policy on the rate of interest will be sufficient by itself to determine an optimum rate of investment. I conceive, therefore, that a somewhat comprehensive socialisation of investment will prove the only means of securing an approximation to full employment; though this need not exclude all manner of compromises and devices by which public authority will cooperate with private initiative. But beyond this no obvious case is made out for a system of State Socialism which would embrace most of the economic life of the community.
>
> It is not the ownership of the instruments of production which it is important for the State to assume. If the State is able to determine the aggregate amount of resources devoted to augmenting the instruments and the basic rate of reward to those who own them, it will have accomplished all that is necessary. Moreover, the necessary measures of socialisation can be introduced gradually and without a break of the general tradition of society.

The tone is calm, and the language is temperate, but the message is breathtaking. It is nothing less than an admission of the practical bankruptcy of any version of capitalism which attempts to limp along as an old-fashioned private enterprise system. The "capitalism" which Keynes envisages must make its peace with a state which exerts a "guiding influence" on consumption and undertakes on its own account a "somewhat comprehensive socialisation of investment." Since consumption and investment in a closed economic system are the components of total spending, Keynes' "capitalism" is translatable into a system in which total spending is directly or indirectly controlled by the State.

How is it possible to term such a resolution of economic impasse "moderately conservative in its implications"? In part, no doubt, because the unstated alternative to such policies is not old-style *laissez-faire* but a "system of State Socialism which would embrace most of the economic life of the community."

The remainder of the answer may lie in Keynes' affection for much that capitalism has achieved and his persistent confidence that reasonable men could combine new economic arrangements with old cultural values. Few defenders of capitalism, and no critic of Keynes of whom I am aware, have so eloquently declared capitalism's values:

> Let us stop for a moment to remind ourselves what these advantages are. These are partly advantages of efficiency — the advantages of decentralisation and of the play of self-interest. The advantage to efficiency of the decentralisation of decision and of individual responsibility is even greater, perhaps, than the nineteenth century supposed; and the reaction against the appeal to self-interest may have gone too far. But, after all, individualism, if it can be purged of its defects and abuses, is the best safeguard of personal liberty in the sense that, compared with any other system, it greatly widens the field of personal choice. It is also the best safeguard of the variety of life, which emerges precisely from the extended field of personal choice, and the loss of which is the greatest of all losses of the homogeneous or totalitarian state. For this variety preserves the traditions which embody the most secure and successful choices of former generations; it colours the present with the diversification of its fancy.

"Purged of its defects and abuses": there's the crux of the matter.[10]

Can a system, recognisably capitalist, endure after defects of income distribution, inadequate investment, excessive saving, and persistent unemployment are removed? How much individualism will remain after a re-distributionist tax system has alleviated the problem of oversaving by diminishing inequalities of income? How much independence of choice will businessmen retain where government intervenes so substantially in the investment process? How much of that variety of life which Keynes enjoyed for himself as much as he cherished it for others can survive in the world of giant organisations?

In America, the doctrinal situation has its ironies. Intelligent businessmen and alert politicians have swallowed Keynesian techniques of monetary manipulation and fiscal adjustment just about the time that these measures have become inadequate to the problems to which they are applied. Although the more radical Keynes who

[10] In recent years Keynes' reputation among Labour Party intellectuals has been somewhat mixed. Titmuss believes that Keynesian doctrine now stimulates social complacency, and offers a "justification for the absence of social protest in our society." More or less in agreement for once, Crossman and Crosland both appear to prefer the Galbraith of *The Affluent Society* to Keynes as a relevant contemporary analyst.

contemplated with equanimity the euthanasia of the *rentier* missed many of the contours of to-day's economies,[11] his conception of social policy seems to have considerable point in a United States whose federal government spends $100 billion or more a year and whose Department of Defense alone disburses between $50 and $60 billion each twelve months.

Increasingly, the real choices of public policy must be made among various versions of private, public, and mixed socialisation rather than between capitalism and state socialism. No socialist, General Eisenhower in his startling farewell remarks to the nation alerted its citizens to the dangers of undue influence from the combination of military officials, defence contractors, and their political allies. Mr. Eisenhower feared that this growingly effective coalition threatened to "involve the very structure of our society." Occasionally truth issues from the mouths of ideological babes. For the General was describing the emergence of highly complex new "compromises by which public authority will co-operate with private initiative." The defence-oriented industries – electronics, missiles, and aircraft – are (in all but name and profit-distribution) government enterprises. The Communications Satellite Corporation, Congress' creation of last year, is a complicated mixture of the private socialism of American Telephone and Telegraph and the public socialism of the federal government. Inadequately, incompletely, and confusingly, the socialisation of investment which Keynes favoured is taking place under a wide variety of auspices.

Even though the main thrust of the volume is in the direction of monetary and fiscal policy, the *General Theory* contains premonitions of this world. But in this latest stage of Keynesian influence the version of Keynes which has become respectable leaves the world more or less as it is. Everybody is a Keynesian now: eminent conservative economists admit as much.

What is needed, however, is a theory to arm the vision of the second, more radical Keynes. Neither Keynes nor anyone else has

[11] But not always. In 1931 Keynes could say: "But more interesting is the trend of Joint Stock Institutions, when they have reached a certain age and size, to approximate to the status of public corporations rather than that of individualistic private enterprises. One of the most interesting and unnoticed developments of recent decades has been the tendency of big enterprise to socialise itself." Keynes' socialism was emphatically non-Marxist: "How can I accept a doctrine which sets up as its bible, above and beyond criticism, an obsolete economic textbook which I know to be not only scientifically erroneous but without interest or application for the modern world." Which may not have been quite the most prescient of Keynes' utterances.

told us how to socialise investment, invent the "compromises by which public authority will co-operate with private initiative," and content all the economic classes. Until a powerful theory emerges, economists will continue to advocate – with decreasing relevance – the policies of the conservative Keynes. How Keynes might have laughed to see the sight.

SUGGESTIONS FOR READING

The General Theory

Serious students will wish to attempt at the least a reading of *The General Theory of Employment, Interest and Money* (1936). Since this book is notoriously difficult in organization and exposition, it might be advisable to study in conjunction with it either:

Dudley Dillard's *The Economics of John Maynard Keynes: the Theory of a Monetary Economy* (1948)

or

Alvin Hansen's *A Guide to Keynes* (1953)

Of the two Hansen offers considerably the more advanced treatment.

Keynes' Life and Opinions

The standard biography of Keynes is Sir Roy Harrod's *Life of John Maynard Keynes* (1951). Harrod, a Fellow of Christ Church College, Oxford, is an admirer and follower of Keynes who in this full biography discusses Keynes' career in public service, his affiliations with the Bloomsbury of Virginia Woolf, Duncan Grant, and Clive Bell, his activities as an entrepreneur of the arts, his notable career as a book collector, all in addition to an analytical account of Keynes' economic opinions and their evolution.

A cool, personal sketch of Keynes is to be found in Clive Bell's *Old Friends* (1956). Bell remembers Keynes entirely in his noneconomic roles.

Keynes himself delivered late in his life a most revealing paper to a small circle of friends. Called "My Early Opinions" it is reprinted in *Essays and Sketches in Biography*, Meridian Paperback, 1956.

This book in its entirety, combined with Keynes' *Essays in Persuasion* (1932) and his still earlier *Economic Consequences of the Peace* (1920), offer a convenient and enjoyable means of learning at first hand Keynes' opinions on a multitude of public issues, among them German reparations and the problems of transferring them to the winning countries, the gold standard, public works as a cure for unemployment, Russian Communism, and English laissez-faire.

Evaluations of Keynesian Economics

Five collections of essays now in print contain in convenient form a very wide range of professional judgments of Keynes and Keynesian influence.

Seymour Harris' *The New Economics* (1947) includes a large number of essays which either evaluate the *General Theory* as a new economic departure, focus on Keynes as an economist, or discuss special aspects of his theories. Although the tone of the majority of the essays is sympathetic and the editor is a leading American Keynesian, a number of critical estimates are also included.

Henry Hazlitt's *The Critics of Keynesian Economics* (1960) is a collection made from a free market standpoint. Here are all the important critics of Keynesian doctrine, among others Jacob Viner, Frank Knight, Arthur F. Burns, and Franco Modigliani, as well as classic names in free market theory like J. B. Say and John Stuart Mill.

Robert Lekachman's *Keynes' General Theory/Reports of Three Decades* (1964) contains nine essays written either in the 1930's or the 1940's and nine new essays by the same authors written in either 1962 or 1963. Prominent Keynesians like Sir Roy Harrod, E. A. G. Robinson, and A. P. Lerner share space with critics of Keynes like Gottfried Haberler, Jacob Viner, and Paul Sweezy.

Gottfried Haberler's readings in *Business Cycle Theory* (1944) contain important essays by Paul Samuelson, John Williams, Bertil Ohlin, John Maurice Clark, Gottfried Haberler, and A. P. Lerner, among others.

Kenneth Kurihara's *Post-Keynesian Economics* (1954) focuses upon contemporary theories of economic growth, based upon Keynesian income relationships. Among the contributors are Dillard, Bronfenbrenner, Patinkin, Klein, and Vickrey.

PB 5156-SB-1